Geezers' Guide
to the Galaxy

A Lifetime of Travel Encounters

Happy Trails,

Jan Burak Schwert

by Jan Burak Schwert

Vashon
Island
Press

Vashon, Washington

ISBN 978-0-9678116-2-8

Vashon Island Press
9609 SW 288th Street, Vashon, Washington 98070
Printed in the United States of America

Praise for
Geezers' Guide to the Galaxy

"In *Geezers' Guide to the Galaxy,* Jan Burak Schwert takes you along on her many adventures, leaving you smiling at the end of every one. She repeatedly gets herself into a fix, but somehow emerges the better for it."

~ Larry Habegger, Executive Editor, Travelers' Tales Books

"Jan's finely crafted, engaging stories highlight the best part of travel, those unexpected moments when we connect on a deeper level with the culture and people of another land."

~ Wendy Hinman, author, *Tightwads on the Loose* and *Sea Trials*

"A wonderful story collection by a veteran traveler and a terrific writer. Join her on an extended romp through North America, Europe and life. Meet the delightful people she encounters, and share the amazing scrapes she gets into... and out of again. You'll be glad you did."

~ Robert H. Mottram, former AP Correspondent; author, *In Search of America's Heartbeat: Twelve Months on the Road*

"With a keen eye for detail and a curiosity that goes beyond mainstream tourism, Jan Burak Schwert weaves colorful characters and an evocative sense of place to explore the deeper meanings of why we travel."

~ Dave Fox, author, *Globejotting: How to Write Extraordinary Travel Journals (and still have time to enjoy your trip!)*

"Jan embraces the risks of the road with the heart of an adventurer. Her vivid writing brings readers along as trusted travel companions."

~ Thomas Kohnstamm, author, *Do Travel Writers Go to Hell?*

Geezers' Guide to the Galaxy

A Lifetime of Travel Encounters

To Ron, for all the perfect moments on and off the road

and Dan, for making me promise to keep on writing.

CONTENTS

How It All Began *v*

1. Ready for Takeoff **1**

2. Flying by the Seat of Our Pants **25**

3. Boy on Board **53**

Introduction

How It All Began

I grew up in the suburbs of Long Island, New York. Happy, secure...and restless.

Every day I'd climb on my horse – an old bike called Trigger rigged with reins and a saddle – and ride for miles, past houses that all the looked the same, then beach shacks, farms and mansions with stables. I talked with strangers and held funerals for dead squirrels on the side of the road.

The only time my family traveled was to visit my grandparents in Rhode Island. My sister and I had to behave and rarely had any fun.

Then at fourteen, I went on a cruise to Bermuda with a friend and her parents. We rode in a jeep with an exotic-looking guide, listened to calypso music and ate fish at a luau. I loved exploring and meeting new people, even dorky grownups in Bermuda shorts. I wanted to keep on traveling and dreamed of being an airline stewardess or a hostess on a cruise ship.

College came first, though, and it was there I began to take risks and have adventures, like climbing out of dorm windows and chugging beer. My motto was "When in doubt, do it."

So a blizzard didn't stop me from driving back to school after Christmas one year, though my old MG had no heat and snow seeped in through the windows.

By the time I got to the Pennsylvania Turnpike I couldn't see past the hood of my car. Gripping the steering wheel tightly, I tried not to skid as I followed the icy ruts made by other vehicles. The only sound I heard was the steady whoosh of the wipers.

After dark a State Trooper pulled me over, said the turnpike was closed and told me to take the nearest exit. Then he sped off. I drove down a ramp until my car got stuck in the snowdrifts.

Fearing I'd freeze in the car, I got out and trudged through knee-deep snow, looking for help. Cold, hungry and surrounded by darkness, I tried not to panic.

A half hour later I spotted a light in the distance and followed it to a farmhouse. Too weak to worry about who lived there, I stumbled up to the door and knocked. A burly man answered. Barely able to speak, I felt relieved when a woman joined him.

"Lord, you look frozen," she said. "Where did you come from?" She rushed me inside, sat me down and served me a bowl of soup. "I'm Arlene, and this here is Bob."

"J-j-an," I said. "Car stuck in snow." The warmth of the house enveloped me like a blanket. My hands and feet began to thaw.

Before long the family gathered for dinner, with eight kids arriving from different parts of the house. Everyone sat down, Bob said grace and they passed around platters of fried chicken and bowls brimming with vegetables and potatoes. The children peppered me with questions and told me stories about lambs, ducks and how to milk a cow in a blizzard.

Bob and Arlene invited me to spend the night. Safe and warm, I slept soundly on their living room couch.

The next day Bob drove me to the exit where I'd left my MG. The roads had been plowed, my car started and I drove back to school. As soon as I got there, two friends pulled me aside, and – breathless with anticipation – said, "What happened to you THIS time?"

Section

1

Ready for Takeoff

I moved to Boston in my early twenties, certain I could do anything and nothing would ever harm me. Every day I'd climb on my Vespa wearing a minidress with heels and putter along fast-moving Memorial Drive. Then I'd stroll into work at the Harvard Kennedy School with a helmet under my arm.

It was the 1960s, a time of assassinations and antiwar protests, but my life revolved around parties, Red Sox games and weekends on Cape Cod.

On a whim I flew from Boston to San Francisco and stayed with a friend in Haight-Ashbury, center of the U.S. antiwar movement and the "Hippie Revolution." Peace activists showed me a more meaningful way to live, and others I met there – fishermen and laborers, musicians and writers – made the soul of San Francisco come alive.

On the way home I stopped in Las Vegas. The contrast in culture stunned me; peace and love had been replaced by noise and vanity. If places and people could vary so much within 600 miles, I thought, imagine how different they'd be around the world. By the end of the trip I knew I'd always be driven to explore new places, meet strangers and learn about their lives.

My passion for travel had been ignited.

Winging It Westward

MY WORLD OPENED UP when I traveled from buttoned-down Boston to free-spirited San Francisco in the summer of 1970.

My friend Richie had bought a Buick from a guy in California. He planned to fly west, pick up the car and drive home by way of Las Vegas, where my roommates Joyce and Karen would be staying.

"Why don't you join the party?" he asked me. "I'll give everyone a ride home."

"Wow, I don't know…I'd love to see San Francisco…."

"Go then. I'll drive you from 'Frisco to Vegas and Karen's father will put us all up." The offer was too tempting to refuse. I got my first credit card – with a $300 limit – and bought a one-way plane ticket to California.

Landing in San Francisco, I had a hundred dollars in my pocket and no place to stay. While looking up the YWCA in a phonebook, I remembered a friend who lived there and called her instead. Kris answered and said I could stay at her place in Haight-Ashbury.

I took a bus to the Haight and found Kris' building. The outside door was open. I walked up four flights of dimly-lit stairs and down a hallway that smelled like mold with an overlay of incense. I knocked on her apartment door.

"Hey, good to see you," Kris said, showing me in. Sitar music played in the background. "I have to go to work – be back about midnight."

"What do you do?" I asked.

"Waitress in the Mission District." She handed me a key. "You can chill in my room," she said, pointing to a doorway with beads hanging down. "There's food in the kitchen. Or check out the neighborhood – it's pretty cool."

"OK, see you later," I said. "Thanks." I put my suitcase in her bedroom and headed out the door.

Within a block I passed people wearing everything from rags to jeans to Hare Krishna robes. In Buena Vista Park, several people with shaved heads chanted in a circle, while others sat by themselves, cross-legged, staring into space. Further down the street I walked by a head shop selling incense and smoking paraphernalia. An old man shouted about God and Santa Claus, and no one seemed to notice. People moved slowly and smiled a lot. I was not in Boston anymore.

Returning to the apartment, I found a map showing all the neighborhoods in the city. I sank into a beanbag chair and studied it. Kris came home about one a.m., saw the map on my lap and said, "You are gonna love this city."

The next day I got up early and went out to explore the city by bus. First stop was the Embarcadero, with its bustling docks, freighters and cruise ships. Teams of longshoremen worked quickly, hauling cargo on and off the giant vessels.

Nearby was Fisherman's Wharf, then a working-class neighborhood with small boats lining the harbor. I bought boiled shrimp from a fisherman and ate them as I walked along, then washed them down with a beer at a local bar.

A man with a weathered face sat next to me. "Where'd you come from?" he asked.

"I've been walking around, looking at the boats," I said. "Do you work on one?"

"Yeah. Done for the day now." His slumped shoulders made him look tired.

Another man walked by. "Catch OK today, Harold?" he asked.

"Oh sure – week's been good on the whole." He turned back to me.

"You live around here?" he asked, signaling the bartender to replace my empty bottle with a full one.

"Boston," I said. "Staying with a friend in the Haight this week."

"Whoa," he said. "Bet you'll see more hippies there than Boston."

He paused. "They're harmless, though. I don't mind 'em."

His words gave me the first hint that people knew how to get along in this city. Later, on the bus, I heard a laborer and a guy in a suit calmly discussing the Vietnam War. That rarely happened in status-conscious Boston.

The following day I wandered through Chinatown to North Beach and the City Lights bookstore, famous since the fifties for publishing Beat Generation poetry and anti-establishment literature. I picked out a Kurt Vonnegut paperback and sat in a corner, reading and watching people squeeze among the book-shelves.

Leaving the bookstore, I smelled pizza baking in a wood-fired oven. Within minutes I was sitting in Tony's, a boisterous, family-run restaurant, savoring a slice and chatting with Tony's mother. Eventually I took the bus home, past colorful Victorian houses overlooking San Francisco Bay.

When I got back, Kris' apartment was filled with people. I plopped down on a couch next to Kris' roommate Tom, whom I recognized from a picture on the fridge.

"Hi, I'm Jan – Kris' friend," I said.

"I was wondering when we'd meet you," he said. "I'm Tom, and that's Rachel over there." She waved. Tom turned his attention to a map laid out on a table. Several people hunched over it, circling parks and street corners.

"Who's covering Dolores Park?" he asked. Someone said he'd do it. "OK, Rachel and I will be at Union Square, and Amy's people will meet in the Castro."

"What are you doing?" I asked.

"Planning protests," said Tom. "Local ones, getting ready for a big rally at the end of the month."

I had seen these events all over the city, peaceful gatherings with people singing, chanting and holding signs opposing the Vietnam War.

The 1960s had been tumultuous, with mass demonstrations across the country for civil rights and against the war. The October 1969 Moratorium to End the War in Vietnam saw millions of people protesting around the country, with a quarter million in Washington D.C. alone. I had gone to that event but hadn't gotten involved at home. My highest goal in Boston was finding the next party.

Now in San Francisco I saw people working together and making a difference; ordinary Americans were paying attention and demanding an end to the war. A demonstrator told me he'd rather do something than stand by and let events roll over him. That made sense to me. By the time I left the city, I vowed to join the anti-war movement in Boston.

Meanwhile, Richie – my ride to Las Vegas – had been staying in the Mission District with his friend George. Late in the week I called to find out when we were leaving. George answered the phone.

"Rich already left," he said. "Told me to tell you to meet him at the International Hotel in Vegas."

"What?" I said, stunned.

"Wait a second…. Here's the number," George said. I hung up, confused. How could he have left me behind?

I called the hotel and got connected to Richie's room.

"HELL-o," he said on the first ring.

"What are you doing there?" I said. "You were supposed to give me a ride."

"Oh, yeah, sorry," he said. "I ran out of money and thought I'd better get here and win some. Didn't have a number for you."

"But I'm in San Fran. How am I supposed to….?"

"Easy. Bus, plane, whatever. We'll wait for you. Call when you know your ETA."

I found a travel agency, pulled out my credit card for the second time and maxed it out with a sixty-nine-dollar plane ticket to Las Vegas. I flew there two days later and Richie met me at the gate. He gave me a big hug, took my bag and steered me towards an exit.

"Jeez, Richie, you could have waited for my call. You said you'd…."

"Hey, you got here, right? Good to see you." His infectious smile made it hard to stay mad at him.

We drove to the Strip, a mishmash of garish buildings, neon, and artificial palm trees. I'd never seen anything like it.

Richie pulled into the driveway of the International, one of the biggest hotels in the world. "Home sweet home," he said. "Go on up while I park – Suite 2411."

I walked through a lobby with fluorescent lights, an orange carpet and green and gold wallpaper. People shouted over the clang of slot machines. Cocktail waitresses in skimpy costumes served drinks at eleven in the morning. Side rooms held dozens of whirring roulette wheels and people crowded around blackjack tables. My brain swirled as I tried to shift from the mellow vibe of Haight-Ashbury to this one.

I took an elevator to the 24th floor and rang the buzzer for the suite. Joyce opened the door and my jaw dropped. The room was enormous.

"Isn't it unbelievable?" she asked as I sank onto a black leather couch. The suite had two levels, a spiral staircase in the middle and turquoise shag carpeting. I expected Liberace to walk down the stairs any minute.

Karen sat in a white velvet chair, sipping champagne, impeccably groomed as always. Joyce chattered away as she led me down the hall. "We have three bedrooms. C'mon, I'll show you ours."

A few minutes later Richie came upstairs. "This is somethin', huh?" he asked me. "You hungry? Here's a menu – order anything you want."

"I'm out of money," I said. "I can't afford…."

"Go ahead," Richie said. "Everything's free. Karen's dad told the manager to take care of us." Her father was a high roller at the hotel's casino.

We ordered a pitcher of whiskey sours followed by steak dinners. Then Richie waited while Karen, Joyce and I got ready to go out. After an hour he said, "Can you wrap it up, girls? Jeez, every freakin' time…c'mon, Joyce."

We made it outside and wandered down the brightly lit Strip. Men in tight bell bottoms strolled by with women wearing furs and flashy jewelry. Car horns and radios blared in bumper-to-bumper traffic. The air smelled of cigars and greasy fried food.

"This place is revolting," I said to Richie.

"Yeah, a little different than San Francisco, right?"

"I'll say." I was appalled by the rude, tacky people and longed for the peace-loving souls I'd left behind.

"I know what you mean," Richie said, walking me into a casino. "People here are ridiculous. Just ignore 'em and have fun."

The casino was quiet compared to the chaos outside. We got free drinks and Richie won $200 at blackjack. I put four quarters in a slot machine and earned three dollars.

The next morning Richie was more chipper than usual. "So, ladies, all set for Elvis tonight?" The King of Rock 'n Roll was headlining at our hotel.

"I don't know," Joyce said. "How much does it cost?"

"Fifteen dollars," Richie said. "But you get two drinks with that."

"Count me out," I said. "I'm down to ten bucks."

"You're NOT missing Elvis Presley," Richie said. "Hell, I'll buy a table for all of us."

"Oooh – seriously?" asked Joyce.

"Sure, I've been lucky downstairs, so…. I'll go buy the tickets right now."

That afternoon Joyce and I watched Karen shop and tried out the pool. By the time we got back to the suite, Richie was decked out in a black suit and red tie, ordering champagne and snacks from room service.

"Any requests?" he asked.

"Caviar!" Karen said.

"Holy s**t," said Joyce.

"Thank god it's free," I said.

We went to our rooms to get ready. Joyce and Karen tried on different outfits while I dug out the only skirt I had with me, an orange nylon one with an elastic waistband. I looked at it and winced; the skirt was way too ordinary for the hotel nightclub.

"I have the perfect top for that," Karen said, holding up a brown silk blouse, beaded on top. "Look, it matches your eyes." The low-cut blouse hid most of my skirt and made me feel elegant.

Dressed up, made up, and hair styled, we gathered in the living room. Richie came out of the bathroom, gasped and staggered at the sight of us. We laughed, drank and ate so many appetizers we didn't need dinner.

At eight o'clock, Richie escorted us downstairs, through the crowded lobby and into the 2000-seat nightclub. He seemed delighted to have three dates. A man in a tuxedo greeted us, and after Richie slipped him a bill he led us to a table about ten rows from the stage.

We ordered cocktails. Richie asked the waitress, "What do you think of the show?"

"Oh there's no one like Elvis," she said. "He can be exhausted or sick and he'll always show up and give a great performance. Every time, the songs sound brand new." I started to feel excited.

A little after nine, spotlights lit up the stage and curtains parted to reveal a full orchestra. A man appeared and announced, "Ladies and gentlemen, Elvis Presley." Cheers went up from the audience.

Elvis walked onstage wearing a white one-piece suit with silver sparkles and a red scarf. His dark pompadour shone, and even from a distance I could see his eyes were a vivid blue.

He went right into "I Want You, I Need You, I Love You" and ended with his trademark "Thankyouverymuch." Some of the women screamed. I couldn't believe I was there.

When the applause died down, Elvis took his guitar and spoke softly into the microphone. "Thank you for being here," he said. "Now I'd like to sing more songs for you." He performed nonstop for over an hour, switching effortlessly from a rollicking "All Shook Up" to the tender "Loving You" to moving gospel hymns like "How Great Thou Art."

At six feet tall, he was a commanding presence and oozed sexuality. Several times he paused to change scarves and tossed the sweat-soaked ones into the audience. Women swooned and the men looked on with admiration. Elvis clearly enjoyed his fans' reactions, but he often looked bemused, as if he didn't take himself seriously.

I was enthralled and moved by Elvis' performance. I had expected a great show but was surprised by his personal connection with the audience. At times he stood alone under a spotlight, singing ballads and playing the guitar. The setting seemed intimate.

During intermission our waitress returned to the table. "Was I not right?" she said, smiling broadly. "Elvis has filled this place every night for three months."

"You're right – this is amazing," I said, turning to Richie. "Thank you so much." He looked delighted that we were enjoying the show. Richie loved to make people happy.

Elvis returned to the stage dressed all in black. He sang for another hour, with more rock numbers and quieter tunes. When he started "Bridge Over Troubled Water," I was sure he couldn't do it justice. But his beautiful voice delivered the song with power and emotion. By the end I could hardly breathe.

After the last note the audience was silent for a moment, and then erupted in thunderous applause. Elvis left the stage, then came back for an encore. The evening was complete.

People filing out of the club seemed spellbound and uplifted. "I've never seen anything like it," one woman sighed.

"He's one of a kind, all right," her partner agreed.

The four of us floated up to our suite and had a nightcap while we talked about the show.

"Maybe Las Vegas isn't so bad after all," I said to Richie, smiling as I headed off to pack.

The next day we climbed into Richie's 1958 Buick and headed home, trading champagne and caviar for fast food all the way back to Boston.

California

Sailors and Banjos

DURING MY FIRST TRIP TO SAN FRANCISCO IN 1970, I set out to find a famous banjo bar called The Red Garter.

I walked through the door at nine o'clock on a Tuesday and the place was jumping. Two men strummed banjos and others played piano, trombone and tuba. I grabbed a seat, ordered a beer and listened to the music.

I hardly noticed when a guy dragged his chair over next to me and sat down, but I soon paid attention. He was slender, a little taller than me, with black, wavy hair. His face opened up with a smile that showed in his deep blue eyes.

He tried to talk over the din. "Hello, I'm Clive. You live in the city?" he yelled.

"No, here for a week, from Boston. Is that a uniform?" He was wearing a dark navy shirt with white trim, some kind of insignia on the shoulder.

"Yeah, I'm a Seaman's Mate on the cruise ship – the one from England."

I nodded and raised my eyebrows, smiling at his accent. As a teenager I'd cruised on the Queen of Bermuda and fallen hard for a British busboy. Clive gestured toward a crowd in the back, all of them wearing the same top and navy pants.

"Wow, that must be some ship."

"We've got a couple hundred crew. Good thing more of 'em aren't here, it's tough finding girls in this place."

I glanced around. It was true, more guys than unattached females. Most of the girls were hunkered down in conversation and didn't seem to want company.

We sat back and listened as the banjos went into high gear, then stopped abruptly for a break.

"They're good, yeh?" Clive said.

"Amazing."

I wanted to hear more about the ship. "So how did you get here from England?"

"Left the UK for the Canaries about eight months ago, then Tunisia and Morocco. Got a break, then sailed for Miami and the Caribbean. Since June we've been cruising up the coast from San Diego."

"Man, what a life. Do they ever hire women?"

"Not for what I do. The only ones on board wait on the passengers."

"Well, why didn't you bring them along?"

"Oh, they don't hang around with us grunts. They've got their own...."

I recognized my mission. "Maybe I can get some of these girls to come over," I said, looking around. It seemed like a waste, so many guys sitting alone and young women all over the room. Besides, I was always up for a party.

His eyes got bigger. "You think you could?" Some of the crew were filing out the door, and he raced off to tell them to wait.

I started talking to the women in twos and threes, gesturing expansively toward the cadre of ready and willing mates smiling expectantly across the room. Most of the girls were happy to join them. We all crammed into large booths at the back.

Pitcher after pitcher of beer was consumed over the next few hours. We sang and cheered loudly at the end of every number. I sat happily next to Clive, who announced at some point, "You've got to see the ship – it's where we all live!" We toasted the Queen of the Seas and kept on laughing.

Closing time was two a.m., and a dozen of us tumbled out of the bar. Most of the group carried on toward a place down the street. But I'd been drinking since five o'clock, and when Clive repeated his invitation to see the ship it seemed a splendid idea to tour it by moonlight. We jumped in a taxi and rode to the Embarcadero.

After stumbling out of the cab, we wound through a maze of warehouses and shipping containers. When he led me up a loading ramp in the dark, it dawned on me that he wasn't supposed to be doing this.

On board, we hustled down a long corridor, the ship rolling back and forth in its berth, waves splashing against the sides. Clive fumbled with his keys and opened the door to a small stateroom with bunk beds and a compact set of furniture: a little desk and chest of drawers, tiny closet, basin in the corner. I vaulted toward the sink, threw up, cleaned up and gargled with water. Then I weaved my way toward the lower bunk and fell face down on the bed. Out cold.

I awoke to blinding light and a stabbing pain behind my eyes. In moments I realized I was on a boat and it was moving. Staggering to the porthole, I saw nothing but water all around.

I collapsed on the little chair, held my head and tried to remember the previous night.

"Jeez, Burak, you've done it this time," I said out loud. "You're probably on the way to China or something." I thought of the friends I'd planned to join for the drive back to Boston and wondered what they'd tell my parents. My face crumpled with tears as I got up and walked in circles around the room.

Suddenly I heard a sharp knock and froze. The cabin door opened slowly. Something was clanking, and a foot and leg came over the threshold.

It was Clive, carrying a breakfast tray.

"Eat this fast," he whispered. "Got to get you off the ship."

"Where are we?" I said, looking up at him. I took some dry toast and waved the rest away.

"Same place as last night, love. Ship's turning around to take on more passengers, some cargo, then we sail. Gotta leave before they need this compartment." He was busy smoothing out the sheets.

"You were a party pooper last night, yeh?" he smiled. "Get your jacket."

The ship's horns were blasting. Clive stuck his head out the door and looked up and down the corridor. We crept along the hall and up a staircase. Emerging on deck, I winced at the bright sunlight and shrank back when I saw well-dressed passengers and crew.

"Shoulders back," he said softly. "You're a visitor and I'm showing you off the ship."

The sea spray felt refreshing, and I was able to breathe again once we got on dry land. Looking back, I admired the sleek lines of the enormous vessel.

Clive put a tenner in my pocket. "For the cab," he said. He gave me a quick hug and said he had to get back. As he walked away, I realized I'd never see him again. I tried to get my hazy brain to tell me what to do.

After a few steps he turned around.

"Can I have your phone number?" he asked. My heart jumped. I rummaged through my purse, looking for a pen and something to write on.

He accepted my scrap of paper and returned my gaze. Then he put his arms around me and kissed me.

He stepped back and cocked his head. "I might get to Boston one of these days. Maybe we can find a good banjo bar there."

"I know just the place."

"Good," he nodded crisply. "That's settled, then."

Clive turned and strode toward the ship. He paused at the gangplank and gave me a little salute, then leapt on board.

I wandered slowly toward a line of cabs. When a taxi door opened, I climbed in and mumbled an address.

"Seeing someone off?" asked the driver, pulling out.

"Yeah, well… I met this guy…."

He shook his head. "Those sailors are hard to pin down."

"I don't know," I said. "This one might be different…."

By the time Clive made it to Boston I was happily engaged to Ron. I enlisted a girlfriend and the four of us went to a banjo bar called Frivolous Sal's. A couple of days later, Clive sailed away.

New York

Bedford-Stuyvesant

SOMETIMES YOU TAKE A TRIP JUST BY GOING TO WORK. That happened to me every time I commuted to my job as a social worker in New York City.

The Department of Social Services (Welfare Department) was always understaffed, with an average turnover of two months. Each social worker was supposed to serve sixty families, but none of us had fewer than a hundred. My beat was Brooklyn's Bedford-Stuyvesant, one of the roughest neighborhoods in the city.

One night, after a fourteen-hour shift and a dozen house calls, I pushed myself to visit one more family. I walked into a crumbling building. It was unlocked and dark inside and the pungent smell of urine almost knocked me over. Taking a few steps, I heard the crunch of cockroaches under my shoes and more scurrying away. The noise of mothers yelling and kids squabbling burst through thin apartment walls.

Light from a single street lamp filtered through a small, grimy window, and as my eyes adjusted I could make out a stairway. I checked my notebook and headed for a third floor apartment.

On the second landing, I almost fell over four or five young men lounging on the stairs. Picking my way through the group, eyes averted, I wondered which guy would expose himself.

But these men seemed engrossed in whatever they were doing and didn't bother me. I walked up another flight, found the apartment I was looking for and knocked. There were noises inside, but no one came to the door.

"Mrs. Smith?" I called out. No one answered. I shrugged my shoulders, jotted a note and went back down the hall. Leaning over the banister, I asked the men, "Has anyone seen Mrs. Smith?"

Some in the group grunted; others said "Nah" or "Not today."

"It's OK, I'll come back tomorrow, I'm just the social worker."

"Ooooh," said one. Another mocked me in a singsong voice, "It's the social worker...."

By the time I got down to the second floor, I saw what they were doing. Two of the guys had pulled rubber tubes tightly above their elbows. Their friends were injecting them with a clear liquid. Needles and glass containers were strewn on the landing.

I started to panic but knew it was hopeless to call out or run back upstairs. I moved slowly towards the men, trying to stay calm as I walked through the group. I was almost past when someone spoke.

"I bet the SO-cial worker never tried this."

"Yeah," said another. "Not the good stuff."

Several got up and moved in front of me. Others followed and went behind.

"You wanna try it? Huh? Huh?"

"I think she wants to try it."

"Yeah, hold onto her and give her some."

They had formed a circle around me that I couldn't break through. One of them grabbed my arm. I was about to start crying but instead became very calm. I planted my feet and spat out words that astounded me.

"HEY, wait a minute, wait a minute. Shut up. You think I'm gonna tell anybody what you're doin' here? Why would I? You don't f*** with me, I don't f*** with you."

The guy with the needle looked stunned, and the one holding my arm loosened his grip. A couple of the others grumbled.

"Hah, lissena her."

"Just do it." The needle came toward me.

All of a sudden, one of the guys raised his voice. "Ah, she's all right. Don' mess wit' her. Break it up, break it up."

I figured he must have been the leader. The circle opened a little. I went through a foot of space, then turned around and looked at them.

"Yeah, well, good. I won't rat on you, you can f***in' count on that." I got to the stairs and backed down slowly, holding the banister in the dim light. By the time I got to the front door, my legs felt like jelly.

I left quietly, ran to the nearest subway station and darted inside. I leaned against a wall to catch my breath. The smell was putrid, the trains deafening, but I felt safe.

After that night I soldiered on, thinking I'd faced the worst my job had to offer. But when I quit two months later, it wasn't the danger that drove me away, but the despair of knowing I couldn't change the system.

Every day I'd trudge from one ruined tenement to another, tracking down my clients and checking on their status. I'd see the same women sitting on their stoops, staring into space, while their children ran around in torn, ill-fitting clothing. Teenagers slouched against buildings, sullen and dejected.

I'd hand out medical information, then learn the clinic I was sending them to had been closed. Lists of job openings I gave them were out-of-date, and when my clients discovered the jobs were gone, they felt helpless and angry. Barely supported by welfare, they were robbed of their spirit and gave little hope to their children.

When I started my job I was just out of college and had high expectations. I wanted to make a difference in people's lives and help those desperately in need. But now I felt my efforts were being wasted and I wasn't helping anyone. Every day I wondered if going to work was worth the risk.

One morning I tried to process a fifteen-dollar shoe voucher for a boy on my caseload who was outgrowing his shoes faster than his family's welfare check could pay for them. As phones rang and typewriters clattered all around me, I tried to complete the many forms required to get him a special allotment. I was almost finished when a policeman appeared beside me.

"Stop what you're doing. There's a lady tearing up the intake office – I need a slip so they can write her a check and get her out of there."

"Who is it?" I asked.

"You know, the Cullen broad. Says she lost her welfare check."

"Again? You know she drank it."

"Yeah, I don't care – just want her gone."

"But..."

My supervisor appeared. "What's going on?"

"I need to get rid of a troublemaker," reported the cop.

My boss looked at me. "Just write him a slip." He turned to go, then glanced back. "Hey, weren't you supposed to be in the field this morning?"

"I was filling out..."

"Leave it, leave it," he said. "Go check on your cases."

Unable to get back to the office for three days, I finally finished my paperwork. A few weeks later I learned that my request had been denied and the boy wouldn't get his shoes. The system had failed again.

I handed in my notice and left the city, still yearning to find a place where I could make a difference.

Section

2

FLYING BY THE
SEAT OF OUR PANTS

WHEN I FIRST MET RON WE DANCED SO HARD the heel of my shoe broke off, which he considered a good sign. After five dates and a week in Vermont we decided to get married, then spent the summer in Europe. We took a charter flight to Amsterdam, picked up a tiny rental car and drove through a dozen countries without a plan.

I felt elated every place we went, from the fjords of Norway to the beer halls of Germany to the chateaux of France. I could barely tear myself away from one country before falling in love with the next. At the end of the trip we decided to live in small houses and drive old cars so we'd always have money for travel.

Ron and I take risks that often lead to detours and surprise encounters. Sometimes I get frustrated or scared, but strangers usually help us, like the farmer in the Scottish Highlands who braved a storm to help us find our B&B.

We find it's the people who make a trip memorable. I'll never forget the old men I comforted in Italy when the Pope died and the scruffy teens in Montenegro who rescued us when we were lost.

By getting to know the locals, we truly experience where they live. And every place we go, we dance.

New York

Driving Lessons

THIRTY MINUTES AFTER RON MET MY PARENTS, we told them we were getting married.

I had driven from Boston to Long Island that day, and Ron had come from Philadelphia. The last part of his trip was on the Long Island Expressway, which had made him frazzled and tense.

"I never saw anything like it," he said. "I thought the Jersey Turnpike was bad."

"Tell me about it." I'd been cowed by the Long Island highway system my whole life.

We were sitting in the living room of the tract house I grew up in, Dad in his recliner and the rest of us on the sofa. The console TV had been turned off, and I could smell Mom's pot roast in the kitchen. After introductions and small talk, Ron and I delivered our news.

My parents looked stunned, but Dad quickly recovered. He jumped up and ran down to the cellar, returning with a dusty bottle of champagne. The wine opened without a pop, but he and my mother were full of good wishes for me and this uptight stranger.

The next morning Ron and I got ready to drive home in opposite directions. We both dreaded getting back on the highway.

"I don't know how I got here, much less the way out," Ron admitted at breakfast.

My father offered him advice.

"When you get to the freeway, take the SECOND on-ramp. Whatever you do, don't take the first one if you want to go west."

"OK," said Ron nervously.

"I'll lead the way," said my dad. "Then I'll get Jan on the Southern State going north."

We left in a three-car caravan: my father, me and Ron. As we approached the Long Island Expressway, Dad and I waved maniacally at the second on-ramp, but Ron had already zoomed onto the eastbound one. My father and I synchronized our U-turns, raced after Ron and got him turned around.

Dad looked at me.

"YOU know where you're going, right?"

"Uh, yeah," I said, after a moment's hesitation.

"Follow me," he sighed.

At the Southern State Parkway, several cars took the southbound entrance, and like a lemming, I followed them. Realizing my mistake, I quickly pulled over. Five minutes later my father came barreling down the road and joined me in the breakdown lane.

He stepped out of his car and walked over to mine, head down, shoulders slumped. I rolled down the window and waited.

He shook his head.

"All I can say is, you deserve each other."

Scotland

Shortbread

IT SEEMED LIKE A FINE IDEA: taking an overnight train from London to Edinburgh to save the cost of a hotel room.

We learned there was only one berth left in the sleeping car, to be shared with another female. I grabbed it, leaving Ron to sleep sitting up in coach class. Before long I was tucking myself into a top bunk and listening to the hum of the wheels as I drifted off to sleep.

At six a.m. a conductor announced the end of the line and brought tea and shortbread to the sleeping car passengers. I sat up in bed and daintily munched my cookies, feeling like a princess.

I had just put down my teacup when I felt the train car backing out of the station. Jumping down from my berth, I got my pants halfway up, grabbed my pack and raced out into the corridor, nightgown fluttering over my unfastened jeans. Ron was running up and down the platform, yelling "Jan! Get off!!" We both knew the train was heading back to London, with me onboard and no way to contact each other.

I was about to leap from the platform when the conductor

intercepted me.

"Oy, Lassie, dunna worry," he said. "We're only switchin' tracks to make way for the next train. Ya can take yur time gettin' yourself together."

The train slowly shifted to the other side of the station. I finished getting dressed, carefully packed up my cookies and disembarked. Ron was there to greet me and I handed him the rest of the shortbread. The conductor leaned out the train window, waving us off.

Scotland

Wrong Station

Ron and I stepped off the train and adjusted our backpacks, ready to walk to our farm B&B about a mile away. It was the summer of 1975 and we were traveling in the Scottish Highlands.

"Uh-oh," said Ron, comparing his scrap of paper with the station name above the door. We'd gotten off a stop too soon.

"When's the next train?" I asked.

Ron looked at the schedule. "Tomorrow – same time." It was six in the evening.

"How far do you think...."

"Pretty far. Maybe fifteen miles or more."

The wind had gotten stronger and the clouds darker. I couldn't imagine hiking in my thin T-shirt and cotton chinos. Ron wore shorts, and we both had lightweight jackets.

We moved back into the depot. Ten minutes later, rain started drumming on the roof. The tiny station, devoid of benches and chairs, smelled of mildew and cow manure. I tried to picture spending the night on the cold wooden floor and shivered at the thought of it.

The room grew darker and damper by the minute; almost no light penetrated its grimy window. We took turns peering out at the soggy grassland dotted with wet, shiny rocks. An empty lane ran along the railroad tracks.

Ron took in a breath. "Is that a truck or a mirage?" he asked. I ran over to the window and blinked.

"Hello," I yelled, leaning out the door.

An old black Ford crawled along the rutted, muddy lane, its load protected by a dirty white tarp. The driver had on overalls and a beat-up cowboy hat.

He stopped and lifted his brim to see us.

Ron poked his head out. "Can you tell me if there's a bus around here?"

"Here? No. We just have the train. Where da ya want ta go?" he asked in his Scottish brogue.

"Beauly," I said.

"Oh, you missed today's train. There'll be another one tomorrow, half past five or thereabouts."

"Yeah, we figured that out. Thanks," Ron said, going back in.

Then he remembered something. Running out to the truck, Ron handed a note to the driver. "Could you call this number and tell the lady we'll be a day late?"

"I could do that," he said. "But…"

Ron was heading back for cover. He looked over his shoulder. "What?"

"Where is it you're spendin' tonight?"

"Um…here," he said.

"Ya better not. Climb in and I'll take ya where you're goin.'"

"Really?" I asked. Ron was already grabbing the backpacks.

We darted out in the rain and squeezed into the cab of the truck. It smelled of hay, stale beer and cigarettes. The driver looked about fifty, with weather-beaten skin and calloused hands. His creased face looked tired.

"Thank you so much," I breathed in relief. "You can't imagine – if you hadn't come along – boy, it was wet in there, and cold...."

Next I would have said, "Do you live around here? What do you farm? Etc., etc., etc." But when I paused for a moment, I noticed the man wasn't responding and didn't seem inclined to chat. Ron and I stayed quiet.

In a half hour or so we turned up a narrow road. The truck hit a pothole, and dirty water sprayed across the windshield. Soon afterward we pulled up in front of a large, light blue Victorian house with a gabled roof, bay windows and a wraparound porch. It looked out of place on the muddy lane.

The door of the house flew open, and a plump woman with white hair and a red face waved us in. I made a run for it as Ron tried to thank the driver and pay him for gas.

Our innkeeper noticed the truck. "Henry? Is that you? Canna give ya a cup o' tea?" She didn't seem surprised at how we got there.

"No thankya," said the man. "Gotta get home now."

"Ah, well, have a safe drive then."

We stepped through the doorway into a homey parlor with over-stuffed chairs lined up before the fire. From the kitchen beyond came the unmistakable, blessed scent of cock-a-leekie soup.

Through the window I could see the truck heading back

down the lane.

"Does he live far?" I asked.

"No, not very," she replied, mentioning the town where we got off the train. Henry had gone over an hour out of his way on that miserable evening to make sure we had somewhere warm and dry to spend the night.

"Imagine him doing that for perfect strangers," I said to Ron.

"Ah, then," our hostess inserted, smiling. "I see you've just arrived in Scotland."

Italy

I'm Not in Love

Ron and I were in northern Italy in August 1980. We had planned to stay in Cinque Terre for two nights, then added another day. Then another. When we finally checked out of our pension, we lingered in the town until early afternoon.

Strolling along lanes edged with bougainvillea, we reached a church sitting on top of a hill. Nearby we saw a small house with a tomato and an olive oil jar stenciled on the side.

I knocked on the door. A middle-aged Italian woman answered, wiping her hands on her apron. Her black hair was tied back and her dark eyes were shining. Ron pantomimed, asking if she had food for sale. "*Bene, bene,*" she said, standing aside so we could enter her small pantry. She pointed to items and raised her eyebrows at us. We said "*Sì, grazie*" to bread, prosciutto, cheese and tomatoes.

After gathering our goods, the woman led us to a small patio below, with two chairs and a table overlooking the sea. She brought us glasses of red wine, then turned on a record player in the corner and left us.

The first song was "I'm Not in Love" by 10cc, one of our favorites since it had come out in 1975. We stood up and danced slowly until the song ended, gazing down at the stunning village and the blue-green Ligurian Sea.

The woman looked out of her window, hands clasped under a radiant smile. We returned to the table and ate her simple, glorious food. Then we told her goodbye, finally ready to say "*Arrivederci*" to Cinque Terre.

Czech Republic

Lost and Found in Prague

RON AND I ARRIVED IN PRAGUE early one Friday evening. We parked our car in the historic center amid seventeenth- and eighteenth-century Gothic and Baroque buildings. Hundreds of vehicles surrounded ours, packed like sardines into every available space.

We walked for more than an hour, looking for a room for the night. Rain pelted the sidewalk as the sky got dark, but we kept on moving. Eventually we found ourselves on a street lined with X-rated shows and "available ladies."

"Want a good time, baby?" someone asked.

"Does that come with a bed?" I wanted to reply.

Hidden among the flashy clubs was the nondescript Hotel Central. As we staggered in, a buxom young woman shimmied by, straightening her dress.

A young man in an elegant gray suit sprang from behind the desk. "Hello, I'm Erik. May I place myself at your service?"

"Do you have a room?" asked Ron.

"Yes, we have one left, but...this hotel may not be right for you."

"Oh, I'm sure it's fine," I said quickly.

"No, you should stay in a more... um... quiet place."

After many phone calls, Erik found a family-run pension near Hradcany Castle that had just had a cancellation. "The owner's daughter is an English translator and will be glad to help you," he said. "But the hotel is difficult to find." That's when we confessed we'd forgotten where we parked our car.

Erik mulled this over. "OK," he said. "I can get you a taxi for 300 *korunas* ($13). The driver will help find your auto, then lead you to the pension."

Soon we heard the roar of an un-muffled engine, accented by clanging and screeching brakes. The ancient vehicle that pulled up outside looked ready to fall apart.

Erik ran out to the cab and leaned on the window, exposing his suit to the rain. He must have explained the situation, but he failed to get much of a response. Finally, with a flourish, Erik held the door open and waved us in.

The driver was draped over the steering wheel, dirty and unshaven, his greasy hair held back in a pony tail. His clothes were ragged and ill-fitting, and the inside of his car was equally unkempt.

"Hello," I said.

"NO ENGLISH!" snarled the man.`

We roared away, careening through streets and parking lots, then dashed down an alley not much wider than the taxi. The narrow street dead-ended, and the cabbie slammed on his brakes, ground into reverse and zoomed backwards.

He sped toward the Charles Bridge. Knowing we hadn't parked across the river, I yelled "HALT!" The driver turned the cab around and, like a homing pigeon, whisked us back to the Hotel Central.

Erik appeared at the car window and spoke to the cabbie, who shouted and gesticulated wildly. Erik returned the barrage of Czech and pounded on the hood of the taxi.

Ron broke in: "That's OK, we'll find our car on foot, then drive to the pension."

"No!" cried Erik. "You'll never find the hotel."

Our friend turned back to the driver, who finally succumbed with a series of resigned grunts.

Once again the cabbie barreled away, retracing the same route. When we got to the bridge a second time, Ron yelled "WAIT!!!"

Suddenly I remembered we had parked near Old Town Square. I found the place on my map and showed it to the driver.

"URNGH!" he said, wheeling the car around.

Many streets radiated from the square. "How will we ever find it?" I asked Ron, peering out the dirt-streaked windows. I couldn't believe my eyes when we went by our Fiat.

"That's it!" I cried. "Stop!" Ron jumped eagerly out of the taxi. But his body slumped when he saw a metal "boot" immobilizing our car and a ticket on the windshield. We looked at the summons. It was in Czech, and we had no idea what to do.

"Urngh – *polizie*," murmured the cab driver, reaching for his cell phone. He made a call and stepped out of the taxi. Leaning on the hood, he sighed and lit a cigarette, despite the steadily falling rain.

I wondered if we had enough cash for a fine. Facing the driver,

I pointed to my wallet and shrugged my shoulders.

The man was indignant. "Urngh!" he exclaimed, writing 300 with his finger on the muddy windshield. "I think he's saying we'll owe him the same amount no matter how long he waits," Ron said, stunned.

Eventually a policeman appeared. His dark, menacing eyes glowered under his officer's hat. He lectured us in Czech, then translated a sign hidden by tree branches: "Private parking." Ron expressed remorse and gave him the 600 *korunas* ($26) he demanded. As we waited for him to unlock the boot, I wondered what we would have done without our cab driver.

We got into the Fiat and followed the taxi, racing down streets, skidding around circles and crossing three bridges. Occasionally we lost sight of the driver, then found him waiting for us up ahead at the side of the road.

When we reached the Castle neighborhood, the cab screeched to a halt. A clock chimed midnight as we crawled out of our cars in the darkness. I saw a light in the pension's lace-covered window.

The three of us stood and looked at each other. I pushed 600 korunas into the cabbie's grubby hand. He shook his head at the extra money, but we refused to take it back. I touched his shoulder and said "Thank you."

The man looked down, then raised his eyes and met mine. He smiled shyly and spoke. "Is super *pension*."

Arizona

Finding Christmas
in the Southwest

IN THE FALL OF 2002, our son Dan, twenty-six, left for a year in Australia and Asia. When Ron and I realized we'd be alone on Christmas, we made plans to spend the holidays out of town. Early Christmas morning we were on a plane, heading for the sunny Southwest.

We had planned the trip around food and unusual places to stay. I had read of a Tucson B&B where guests felt like they were sleeping in a folk art gallery, and a nearby Mexican restaurant called Cafe Poca Cosa, "an authentic, family-run place with the best mole sauce in the country." Ron had heard on the radio about Bisbee, Arizona, where you could stay in an Airstream at the Shady Dell Vintage Trailer Park and eat "the world's best pot roast" at Dot's Diner.

Ron and I arrived in Tucson at seven p.m. Christmas night. The city was dark but for the *luminaria* outside many homes and churches. I noticed all the restaurants were closed, so we bought snacks and canned margaritas at a gas station. We drove around Old Town until we saw a dimly lit adobe building with faded writing on the side: Elysian Grove Market – now home to our B&B.

Desert plants hugged the outside walls, and two six-foot-tall cacti stood like sentries guarding a weathered grey door. Fresh holly tied with red ribbon decorated the entry. A light above the front door meant we hadn't been forgotten. I reached in the mailbox and found a key.

When I opened the door, a spacious room took my breath away. Southwest folk art – paintings, ceramics, handmade creches – decorated walls and tables under vaulted ceilings. Candles graced every surface, waiting to be lit. A soft leather couch and chairs with red and turquoise pillows encircled a cast iron fireplace.

We went down a stairway and found the master bedroom, full of metal-framed mirrors and handwoven baskets. Dropping our bags, we returned to the living room. I lit the candles and Ron started a fire.

I recalled what I'd read about our B&B. The Elysian Grove Market in the *Barrio Viejo* ("old neighborhood") had been renovated about ten years earlier and turned into two apartments. Karen, the owner, had said we could stay in the larger one for a night, then switch to a smaller apartment so a group of six could stay in this one.

Ron and I ate our snacks and margaritas for Christmas dinner, sitting on the sofa in front of the fire. I missed our usual roast beef and Yorkshire pudding, but without the distractions of preparation and cleanup, Ron and I could enjoy our surroundings while sharing memories of past Christmases.

"Remember Vermont, when the power went out?" Ron said. "I think we were snowed in."

"Thank God for wood stoves. But outside it was magical," I sighed. "So quiet."

"As opposed to Buffalo with my relatives," said Ron.

"Daniel loved the chaos," I remembered. "Wonder what

he's doing tonight?"

"I don't know," said Ron. "Probably having a meal like this one."

We explored the rest of the apartment. A large dining table and chairs filled one end of the living room. Open steel doors to the kitchen suggested it had once been a meat locker. Inside, green kitchen shelves held dinnerware painted with orange poppies.

I made dark cocoa Southwest style – with a dash of chili powder. Returning to the couch, we watched the crackling fire until bedtime. The pleasing scent of snuffed-out candles followed us to our room.

The next morning we met Alison, who was there to cook our breakfast.

"Nice to meet you," I said. "Is Karen around? I enjoyed talking with her on the phone."

"No, she's in Puerto Vallarta finding furniture and art for a place she bought down there," said Alison. "I'm taking care of the B&B while she's gone."

Soon the spicy aroma of eggs and salsa drew us to the table, where Alison set down plates of *huevos rancheros* and fresh corn tortillas. At the end of the meal, she joined us for a cup of coffee.

"This place is amazing. Hard to believe it was a market," I said. "Do you know what it looked like?" The space must have bustled with barrio neighbors buying groceries and sharing gossip.

"I do – in fact, we have pictures." She led us to a narrow hall near the back door. On the wall were black and white photos of men in aprons standing outside in front of the market.

"These were taken in the 1920s," said Alison. One side of the building was open so produce could be displayed. Inside, dry goods and hardware filled a cavernous room. The meat locker was at one end of the market.

We stared at the pictures, trying to see where Karen had divided the space. "I understand we're moving to another room today," Ron said. "You're expecting a large group here?"

"Yes," said Alison. "Six men visiting from Italy." She showed us to a smaller suite, also filled with antiques and art.

After moving to the other rooms, we drove to the Arizona-Sonora Desert Museum. The 100-acre facility preserves habitats for 1200 kinds of plants and 300 animal species, many of which are endangered. Ron and I wandered for hours among giant Saguaro cacti and tiny wildflowers.

We headed back to Tucson for dinner at Cafe Poca Cosa. Lively music played and the owner welcomed us warmly. Patrons of all ages sat at tables with bright yellow linens and vases of desert flowers. We feasted on perfectly cooked, spicy-sweet chicken mole.

Returning to our bed and breakfast, we saw the group of men had arrived. They were outside talking loudly in Italian while their English-speaking guide spoke to Alison.

"They don't speak English," he told her, "but they should be OK until I come back tomorrow. If you need me, I'll be home all evening." He gave her a card, climbed into his van and left.

We slept well that night in our four-poster bed, then woke up and made coffee. Alison dropped by with omelets stuffed with fresh vegetables. We were almost finished when she burst back in the door. She was frantic.

"Do you know how to fix a water pipe?" She looked beseechingly at Ron, whose lack of experience with house repairs was surpassed only by my own.

"No, I don't," he said. "What's happening?"

"I think a pipe burst. There's a fountain of water...oh god...can you come over?"

The three of us bolted out the door, around the corner and into the back yard. Old Faithful shot up from the roof and our new neighbors were tearing around, broadcasting panic in a cascade of Italian.

"I think you'll need a wrench," offered Ron. Alison and I went inside and searched madly through kitchen drawers.

"I don't even know where the pipe is," she wailed.

Back outside the men still raced back and forth, ducking under bushes. The loud stream of Italian never stopped.

"Hmmm," said Ron. "I wonder if there's a shutoff valve...."

At that moment one of the men dropped to his knees and reached forward. I heard metal scraping on metal. The geyser disappeared. We all cheered and the Italians clapped their hero on the back.

Alison came out, holding a wrench. She looked bewildered.

"One of the guys found the shutoff," said Ron.

"Thank goodness," she said. "I'll call a plumber."

We went inside and got ready to leave. "Those guys are a riot," I said. "Wish I had seen their faces when the pipe burst."

As we put our bags in the car, Alison came to say goodbye. "A repairman is on the way over," she said, "and so is the tour guide. The Italians are moving on today."

"Bet you'll be glad for a little peace and quiet," I said.

"I will," she replied, laughing.

Soon we were on the highway, driving through desert sagebrush country with mountains looming in the distance.

In a couple of hours we pulled into the Shady Dell Vintage Trailer Park, where we would stay in a restored Airstream and eat at the famous Dot's Diner.

I had reserved a seventeen-foot El Rey model crafted in 1957. The compact trailer had black and white checked linoleum floors and a breakfast booth with red vinyl seats. A Mixmaster and percolator sat on the counter, and blond wooden cabinets held Melmac dinnerware.

After a delicious pot roast dinner at Dot's, Ron and I settled into the trailer to play cards and listen to fifties music on the radio. I felt snug in our cozy Airstream as we stepped back in time.

We spent the next few days looking around Bisbee, an old mining town that had morphed first into a hippie colony, then an artist's enclave. A highlight was exploring the tunnels of a copper mine that had produced ore for 100 years before closing in 1975.

On our last morning I woke up to the sound of Ron yelling: "It's the Italians!" He pulled on his pants and stumbled out the door. I was right behind him.

Ron raced over to greet the men, but they didn't seem to recognize him. He waved his arms wildly in curved, upward motions, crying "Whoosh! Whoosh!," trying to imitate a geyser.

The guide stood between Ron and his group, protecting them from this lunatic. Then Ron explained where he'd met the Italians. The guide looked doubtful, but he translated what Ron had said. In a few seconds, they shouted, "Ahh, *sì! sì!*" as they smacked their foreheads and broke into brilliant smiles.

"Don't tell me," their leader said. "You're going to the Grand Canyon next, right?"

"Nope – you're on your own," Ron replied. The men filed over to their van, shaking their heads and laughing.

Later that day Ron and I reflected on the week, and on surviving Christmas alone. Our family was changing, and we had flown away to escape that reality. But in fact the trip had been exhilarating.

Ron and I would remember Arizona as the place where we started the next phase of our lives.

France

Running the Rapids

OUR PASSPORTS HAD BEEN STOLEN IN BARCELONA, and we weren't about to let that happen again.

It was the summer of 2003, and Ron and I were staying in St. Etienne, France. Kayakers dotted the Tarn River, paddling under cliffs crowned by sixteenth-century stone buildings. The boats were painted red, yellow and green.

We watched the scene and decided to try paddling ourselves. "But I'm not leaving our stuff in the car," Ron said.

"Yeah...remember what happened to Madeleine and Fred."

A couple we'd met in Nice had rented jet skis there. When the ride was finished they went to their car and found their backpacks were gone.

We rented a canoe from a kiosk near the river. An attendant gave us a small plastic barrel to carry our valuables during the ride. We put our passports, wallets, camera, keys and watches inside, along with a bottle of water and granola bars.

Ron placed the barrel in the back of the canoe and shoved the boat into the water. We climbed in, pushed off and paddled down the river. After ten or fifteen minutes we saw a few ripples, then went over a tiny waterfall.

Our boat bumped against a log, moved sideways, hit the bank and turned over, spilling us and the barrel into the shallow water. Our valuables went floating down the river. I held onto the canoe while Ron ran after the container, slipping and falling on the rocky river bottom. With a final burst of energy and a giant leap, he grabbed the barrel by one of its straps.

Mission accomplished, he began limping back up the river on one flip-flop, pulling the barrel behind him. Suddenly it hit me: we were supposed to use the straps to tie the container to the canoe. When he reached the boat, we secured the barrel, climbed aboard and paddled down the river to meet a truck that would take us back to town.

Neither of us told the driver about our close call, which Ron still refers to as "running the rapids" in France.

Section

3

Boy on Board

Our son Daniel was born in 1976. Ron and I vowed not to take him to Europe until he could stay amused on a plane for ten hours. Still, we never stopped traveling. Dan took his first road trip from Vermont to Milwaukee at age three months and flew cross-country twice before his fourth birthday.

He was five when we quit our jobs and moved to Seattle. We celebrated living in the Northwest, camping across British Columbia and driving along the coast of Oregon and California.

At nine, Daniel was ready to fly across the Atlantic. We spent a month exploring England, Belgium, Switzerland and more, exposing him to the history and culture of Europe while having a lot of fun.

Our travel style didn't change much. We still stayed in people's houses and ate local food, but now the three of us planned trips together and took turns choosing what to do. Dan sat through a concert in Bruges, then led us on a search for Manneken-Pis, the statue of a little boy peeing into a fountain. He was patient as we explored a London market, looking forward to the "Jack the Ripper" tour he'd picked out for that night.

I knew we had raised a good traveler when fourteen-year-old Daniel, Ron and I stayed at the Corner House in Dingle, Ireland. One day at breakfast our hostess, Mrs. Farrell, leaned over, hands folded, and said, "Can I ask ya a question?"

"Sure," I said.

"Well, I'm just wonderin' now. How is it your son is such a civilized child, being an American?" I had never felt prouder.

Dan finished college with a Semester-at-Sea voyage to developing countries around the world. In his twenties he backpacked for six weeks in Europe. And he took what he called his "first retirement" at age twenty-six, traveling for eight months through Australia, Thailand and Cambodia.

Ron and I are thrilled that he shares our love of travel.

Washington

Secondhand Jack

LOCAL LORE SAYS LA CONNER IS ALL ABOUT LOVE. It started with the love of a husband, John Conner, who named the Skagit Valley town for his wife, Louisa Ann Conner.

The small town lies an hour north of Seattle. Tourists flock there in the spring to see vast fields of tulips in bloom or view thousands of migrating snow geese that lie so close together the fields turn downy white.

One day, when a pale sun followed weeks of rain, Ron, nine-year-old Daniel and I decided to head for the country. We were off to La Conner to get ice cream at the Calico Cupboard Café.

Strolling along First Street, we passed gift shops and fabric stores and the town's compact Museum of Northwest Art.

A scruffy little dog trotted out of the antique shop ahead of us.

"Look at him," said Ron. "He looks like he belongs in a secondhand store."

"I see what you mean," I said.

The pup reminded me of a dog I'd seen in an old children's book. A border collie runt, his matted black coat and white markings were almost hidden under a layer of dirt. But as

I watched him bounce along the sidewalk with his grimy, white-tipped tail waving freely back and forth, I could tell he was an optimist.

Ron and Daniel followed me into the shop. "That's a good-looking dog you have," Ron said to the man behind the counter.

"Good-looking?" Daniel questioned, glancing at me. I shrugged my shoulders.

"Ain't my dog – been around all week. Don't know where he come from – maybe the reservation," said the storekeeper, referring to nearby lands belonging to the Skagit tribe. "He probably just wandered away, and nobody tried to find 'im."

Ron tore out the door. Dan and I peered down the street to see him a block away, running after the stray. He caught him, scooped him up and brought him back to the shop.

"Can we keep him?" pleaded my husband.

Before that moment, we had no intention of getting a dog.

"I don't know, Ron, what about Robin?" I figured our twelve-year-old cat wouldn't approve.

"They'll get along, I know they will." The puppy looked at me with his big brown eyes, as if he knew what we were talking about.

"Ya know, Dad," said Daniel sternly, "a dog's not like a cat, you have to walk him, wash him, take him to parks...." How does he know all that? I thought. We've never had a dog. But he was right about the washing – the animal was a mess.

"I'll take care of him," Ron promised.

Daniel and I looked at each other in dismay, trying to come up with more arguments. The pup eyed one of us, then the other. I started to relent. "Well, if you really think...."

Daniel began petting the puppy. "Just remember, Dad, you're the one who's gonna take care of him."

"I know. I will," said Ron.

"Guess we've got ourselves a dog," I told the storekeeper, leaving our name and number in case someone claimed him.

"That's a good thing," the man answered. "Little guy's been bullied pretty bad by the bigger strays." I pictured the brave puppy struggling on the streets of La Conner. All of a sudden I wanted him, too.

Forgetting about the ice cream, we headed for our car. Once inside, the muddy dog curled up on my lap and let out a weary sigh, as if he knew he belonged there.

We called him Jack, after the dog in "Little House on the Prairie," and all three of us took care of him. Clearly, we came to agree, the town of La Conner is all about love.

Italy

This Ain't Venice Beach

Few locals knew English in Cinque Terre, but when I needed help, a handsome Italian spoke my language.

It was the summer of 1992 when Ron, teenage son Dan and I spent a week in Cinque Terre ("Five Lands") on the northwest coast of Italy. The region is made up of five ancient towns perched on the tips of five peninsulas that reach into the Mediterranean like an outstretched hand. We were staying in Riomaggiore, the southernmost village.

Cinque Terre towns are filled with crumbling pastel buildings that tumble down to the sea. Hundreds of years ago, Italians hauled materials across rugged terrain to build their houses against the rocky hillsides. The pluck needed for such a feat can still be seen in the people who live there. Ninety-year-old women move quickly up and down the steep streets, leading their great grandchildren by the hand. Villagers are raised and lowered in buckets, a dozen hours a day, to harvest grapes on the narrowly terraced hillsides. Fishermen work from dawn to dusk to make a living from the sea.

The five villages are connected by a two-car, hundred-year-old train and by rugged paths that lead from one town to another. Hikers on the trails can scramble down to refresh themselves in the clear, azure water.

One hot, sunny afternoon, the three of us hiked north a few miles from Riomaggiore to the village of Manarola and the narrow boat ramp just beyond. It was surrounded by large flat-topped rocks, perfect for sunbathing.

As we spread our towels, a couple emerged from the sea, and I couldn't help but stare. The man, just over thirty, was movie star gorgeous, about six feet tall and slim with a tanned, muscular body. His shiny dark hair fell across his face when he leaned over to talk with his young girlfriend, another stunning brunette. They lay down on the other side of the ramp, talking softly in Italian as the girl removed her blouse. Ron and Dan glanced over, then turned and went to sleep; even our sixteen-year-old had grown blasé about topless women.

I took a short nap and woke up feeling hot. Stripping down to my bra and shorts, I slid down the rocks into the cool, soothing water. I paddled out and floated with my eyes closed, feeling the warmth of the sun. After drifting far from shore, I turned around and swam back.

I made it to the boat ramp, but every time I tried to get out, small, insistent waves knocked me off balance. Finally, I lunged forward and grabbed the edge of the ramp with my left hand. To my surprise, someone grasped my right one and pulled me up.

"This ain't Venice Beach," he said, without a trace of an Italian accent. It was the handsome thirty-year-old, who had seen that I was in trouble. "My name's Tom," he said. "Hi."

My voice came out shakier than usual: "Oh...ah, hi...thanks. I'm, uh, Jan." He flashed me a dazzling smile, which faded quickly when he looked at my left hand. I gasped to see blood flowing heavily from a deep cut in my palm.

Tom dragged me up the ramp, wrapped my hand in a towel

and helped me clamber over the rocks, muttering about sharp coral. "She needs help," he yelled to Ron and Dan, waking them up. They grabbed our stuff and followed behind, barely keeping up as Tom and I raced back to Manarola. Tom's girlfriend brought up the rear, her top half-buttoned.

"Where are you staying?" asked Tom, as Ron helped me put on my blouse.

"Riomaggiore," I replied, catching my breath. "The Argentina Hotel."

When we reached the village, Tom led us into a newspaper shop where, after a few words from Tom, the storekeeper produced a phone book. Tom called a physician in Riomaggiore, spoke with him in rapid Italian, listened carefully, then hung up the phone and turned to me.

"You need to take the train to Rio'," he instructed, pointing to the tracks. "Keep the towel pressed on her hand," he told Ron. "The doctor will be at your hotel when you get there."

I was grateful for his help, but he waved away our thanks. "Glad I could help."

I started down the street, then looked over my shoulder. "Where are you from?" I asked. "Atlanta," he replied with another bright smile.

The train came quickly and we reached our town in a few minutes. Ron and Dan helped me climb the steep hill to our hotel.

Il medico arrived right after we did. A distinguished, grey-haired man of about seventy, he wore a crisp white linen suit and carried a black leather doctor's bag like you see in old movies. He seemed reserved, yet I felt comfortable with him, even when he said "*quattro suturare*," which meant I needed stitches. He spoke to the hotel owner, who turned to me and said, "You go to *clinica*, five o'clock. Above *farmacia*."

The physician wrapped my hand, then left on other business. Ron, Dan and I walked down the hill to find something to eat. In a quiet cafe, they both had spaghetti, but all I could manage was soup. The fragrant minestrone gave me comfort but couldn't dispel my sense of dread as my appointment drew near.

We walked to the center of the village where I saw a sign: *Farmacia*. Looking up, all I could see was a woman hanging out laundry. I smiled and spoke: "*Scusi, dové la clinica?*"

She waved us up, pointing to a stairwell on the side of the ancient building. It was dark, with steep stone stairs that were crumbling. I felt as if I were on the set of *Cinema Paradiso*.

At the top of the stairs a single door was open and the three of us walked in. Half a dozen people, mostly elderly, were lined up on benches in the stark, white room. "*Scusi,*" I said, taking a seat; Ron and Dan remained standing. Periodically the doctor came out of his office to beckon in his patients, one at a time or sometimes in pairs. Several came out of his office quickly, clutching pills, while others took longer.

After about forty minutes the physician motioned us in. Ron and I entered the tiny office, which held a bed, two metal folding chairs, a table spread with instruments and shelves filled with liquids, powders and pills.

The doctor looked down at my hand. "*Oh, Meekey,*" he said, seeing the bloodstains on my Mickey Mouse watch. He applied disinfectant to the palm of my hand and threaded what looked like a large sewing needle with thick black thread. I glanced nervously at Ron when I saw no sign of an anesthetic.

When the needle plunged into my hand, I grimaced but didn't make a peep, calling up my mother's admonitions to be brave in the doctor's office. He hummed as he worked, and I told myself that someday this would make a good story. Finally he knotted and snipped the thread, then bent down and swept cotton and thread into a dustpan. Ron looked pale but relieved.

Suddenly I thought of something. Looking at the doctor, I formed my face into a question and moved my arms as if swimming. He shook his head firmly: "No." I promptly held the injured hand up in the air and stroked with the other. The physician turned his wrist back and forth: "Maybe."

Satisfied, I gave him a smile, then said: "*Il costo?*" He grabbed a piece of paper and wrote, "50,000 *lira*."

"Only fifty dollars," Ron said, taking out his wallet. "Imagine that."

The doctor wrote something more, then pointed to my hand and made a snipping motion with his fingers. Later I looked up what he had written: "Stitches come out in two weeks."

"*Grazie,*" I said. "*Arrivederci.*" As we picked up Dan in the waiting room and went downstairs, my knees felt weak. We made it to the nearest café, where Ron and I ordered shots of grappa to calm our nerves.

Over the years the scar has faded and I barely recall the trauma, but I'll always remember being rescued by a handsome stranger.

Bahamas

Flashback

IN JANUARY 1999, TWENTY-TWO-YEAR-OLD DAN took a Semester-at-Sea voyage to third-world countries around the globe. Ron and I flew to the Bahamas to see him off, calling it "parental sacrifice" as we left the drizzle of Seattle for a week in the sun.

The morning he was to set sail, we took Dan out to breakfast and drove him to the docks. Even while sharing his excitement, I felt anxious about the trip. As we bounced along in our rented jalopy, I wanted a distraction and tried for the umpteenth time to get the radio working.

Our son's ship loomed ahead when the radio finally sputtered to life. Elton John's voice filled the air: "I can see Daniel waving goodbye."

The moment reminded me of a crisp, fall day more than twenty years earlier, when Ron and I lived in the foothills of Vermont's Green Mountains. Our farmhouse was surrounded by verdant hillsides and cornfields. The only neighbors were three Holstein cows who would lean over their fence and peer into our sitting room.

That particular day I tore down our driveway, kicking up leaves in my bus-yellow Hornet. The cows glanced up, surprised.

When I reached the house, I jumped out and sprinted through a curtain of dust to look for my husband.

Ron had been out patching our chimney when his mug fell off the ladder. He'd gone inside for a refill and turned on the radio.

I saw him through a window and raced in to make my announcement.

"You don't have to say anything," he said. "Just listen to the tune." Anne Murray was singing the first few notes of a song as I came through the door.

"And we've just begun. I think I'm gonna have a son. He will be like you and me, as free as a dove. Conceived in love...."

I nodded, and tears spilled from my eyes.

The following April Dan was born, and years later I learned that the tune we'd heard on the radio that day was called "Danny's Song."

Now, hearing "Daniel" on the car radio, I remembered other times when music had come with a message. As my son reached forward and squeezed my shoulder, I felt sure that whoever had put his life on a sound track would watch over him and keep him safe until his return.

Section

4

Finding Adventure in Business Travel

During the 1980s and '90s, I worked at the University of Washington and traveled to conferences several times a year. These trips were chances to explore new places, and I made the most of them.

Many of my colleagues stayed where meetings were held – usually in chain hotels – while I opted for small inns or funky B&Bs. I researched destinations, made lists of places to go and marked them on a map. Conference friends relied on me to locate good Irish pubs and venues that played oldies music.

At the end of every day I couldn't wait to shed my work clothes, put on jeans and find a hole-in-the-wall restaurant. I'd think of my colleagues talking business in a hotel dining room as I happily drank beer and hammered crabs with newly-made friends. Even in dicey neighborhoods, I could find someone interesting to talk to. Then, after the conference, I'd stay a few extra days and explore places like the swamps near New Orleans or Mt. Denali in Alaska. It was easy to meet strangers on a twelve-hour ride in a two-car train from Anchorage to Fairbanks.

Ron encouraged me to take advantage of these trips, though his work as a teacher prevented him from joining me. At times I felt guilty for deserting him and Daniel. Once I asked if they minded my being away. They glanced at each other and Ron said, "Well, it makes for a change."

That's when I realized how much they liked spending time on their own. Dan and Ron were fine while I was gone, and I felt free to enjoy wherever my travels took me.

Texas

Honeysuckle Rose

I'VE ALWAYS BEEN A WILLIE NELSON FAN. So the first time I traveled to Texas I headed straight for Austin and the Broken Spoke, Willie's local hangout. When the singer didn't stop by, I had to settle for some black and white photos on the wall.

From there I drove to San Antonio for a conference, where I was cooped up all week, gazing out the window at boats sailing along the river. As soon as the meetings were over I hopped on a bell-clanging trolley to see the rest of the city, including Old Town and the King William Historic District.

My walking map of King William showed its many Victorian mansions, stunning houses painted in sherbet colors with spacious lawns and fountains, beveled doors and lace-covered windows. I took dozens of pictures and used up my film. Little did I know how much I'd need it later.

At the edge of the neighborhood I saw a dilapidated bus that had seen better days, probably carrying rambunctious children on their way to school. But now it looked worn and battered, like a broken toy tossed against the curb. I could barely make out the letters painted on the side next to a few music notes and a fiddle: H-o-n-e-y-s-u..."Honeysuckle Rose."

I stopped and stared. "Wait a minute," I said to myself.

"Could that be.... No." But I knew Willie Nelson had a record called "Honeysuckle Rose."

I crossed the street and talked to a young man standing in front of a restaurant. "That bus doesn't have anything to do with Willie Nelson, does it?" I asked.

He raised his head briefly. "Yeah," he mumbled. "He's in the bus."

"In the bus." I took a moment.

"Can I go in there?" I asked, trying to sound casual.

"Nah," he said. "His lawyer's inside."

The man looked to be in his early twenties. He wore shapeless jeans and a flannel shirt over a faded blue T-shirt. Shaggy hair obscured his face as he looked down and scraped the ground with his cowboy boots. When he raised his head, his right eye focused on me while the left one strayed to the side. I wondered about his eyes, then followed the left one to an old guitar leaning on a bench.

I looked at the instrument, glanced at him again. My head jerked back as I realized where I'd seen the guitar – draped on Willie during all of his concerts over the past few decades. There was no mistaking the worn red, white and blue strap, the signatures carved in the battered wood.

"So that's...."

"Yup. I'm supposed to guard it."

I leaned over the guitar and examined the names. "Johnny Cash" stood out more than the others. "Wow, that must be worth a lot."

"They say when Willie goes it'll fetch millions." He moved it to the shade and I saw his hands were shaking. Slouching and slight of frame, he seemed an unlikely bodyguard.

"How long will he be?" I was cutting it pretty close already; my plane was leaving in a couple of hours.

"Not sure, maybe thirty, forty minutes?"

"Maybe I can wait…but I'll need film. Any idea where I can buy some?"

"Naw, we just been here a few hours. Don't know the neighborhood – or the town, really. Austin's where we hang out."

"I'll be right back."

I sprinted across the street and darted into a little store. Displays of tiny silver charms in the shape of body parts covered the walls. I recognized them as *milagros*, Spanish for miracles. According to Mexican folklore, if you need help with something you can attach a charm to a favorite saint's icon to remind him of your need – a tiny arm to heal a broken one, a heart for romance. If only I could find a little cowboy hat, I thought, I could pray to meet Willie.

Behind the counter was an elderly man whose small facial features and tiny hands seemed custom-made for the shop. Engrossed in examining miniscule heads and feet, he had no idea I was there.

"Excuse me…." He jumped a little and drew back. "Do you sell film by any chance?"

"No, no, you'll have to go to the Circle K, maybe half a mile down that-away." I left the store and started in the direction he'd pointed, then paused and re-crossed the street, so distracted by my dilemma that a car had to brake and swerve around me. The guitar guy was still there, steadily looking after the instrument.

"So, d'ya think I can meet Willie when he comes out?"

71

"Pro'bly...well, I don't know for sure. But he has to walk right by here, and acourse he needs his guitar...."

"What's going on, anyway?" I asked as people carried equipment into the building.

"José Cuervo ad. In the restaurant." He nodded toward a small hacienda with potted fuchsias decorating the porch. I peeked in the door and saw bright green and yellow banners and piñatas hanging from the ceiling.

A man walked into the restaurant with a large camera. I pounced when he came back out. "Can I buy a roll of your film? I used mine up and just found out Willie Nelson's in there and I always wanted to meet him and...." I waved my Canon point-and-shoot.

"I'd love to help you, little lady, but I don't think.... lemme see that camera," he said. "Yup, my film won't work in there. I've got a whole different setup. Wait, I'll ask a couple...."

He went inside and hollered, "Anybody have any 35mm film on 'im? Lady out there wants...." A bunch of murmurs, none in the affirmative. He poked out his head. "Sorry."

My face fell. I yearned for a picture of Willie and me, but if I left to buy film I might miss him entirely. So I lay down on a bench next to the restaurant and practiced what to say. I promised myself I'd speak slowly for once in my life.

About twenty minutes later, I heard the bus door open and saw Willie walk down the steps and squint in the sunlight. He was duded up for the shoot, trademark red railroad scarf, hair tied neatly in braids, cowboy hat in place. He strode toward the restaurant, and my new friend left the guitar to intercept him. I saw him point at me, tilt his head and whisper. "She's been here...."

Willie walked toward me and I was struck by how small he was, no taller than my 5'5" and lighter in weight. His face looked old and weathered, peaceful and calm. He stood a foot or two in front of me, held out his hand. I shook it, and he closed his palms around mine. His skin felt warm and rough.

"Hello," he said. I'm Willie Nelson."

No kidding, I said to myself.

"I'm, uh, Jan, and...I, ah, I'm glad to meet you. I've b-been a big fan of yours for...I mean, I love your music, your, um, your style." You're blowing this, I thought.

"Well, that's good to hear. Do you live in the area?"

"No, I'm, ah, here for work – a conference...."

"Nice place, San Antonio."

"Yes and, well...." Remember what you wanted to say, I told myself. "I, um, I wanted to tell you how g-great...I mean, what a great job you've done with, uh, Farm..., you know, for the farmers."

He seemed in no hurry to leave, just stood there waiting for me to finish. But one of the cameramen called him over.

"Well, it's been real nice to meet you," he said.

"Me too," I responded feebly.

Willie saw the walking map in my hand. "Would you like me to....?" he asked softly. I nodded and gave him the map; he wrote something down. Then he turned around and walked into the restaurant. An idiotic grin froze on my face.

Just then a cab appeared. I leapt inside, flashed a smile at my guitar man and zoomed off toward the hotel. Flying past the front desk, I paused long enough to show them my walking map: "To Jan, Love, Willie."

I stared at his name most of the flight home and spilled the story to Ron the minute I saw him. He shook his head.

"Texas is a very big state. How in the world did you end up on the same block as Willie Nelson?"

"Probably because I wanted it so much."

"Did you get your picture with him?"

"Out of film." But I didn't need a photograph. The memory, as the song says, will be always on my mind.

Alaska

The Bird House Bar

"You're going to Anchorage?" asked a friend in Seattle. "Be sure and get to the Bird House bar."

"OK. Where is it?" I asked.

"In Bird Creek, about thirty miles south of the city. Take the highway toward Seward – it's pretty hard to miss."

I decided to check out the bar on the way to Portage Glacier one morning. I drove along the shore of Turnagain Arm, where dramatic views of the mountains and water make the route from Anchorage to Seward one of the most scenic in America.

On a previous work trip to Anchorage, I had walked on a beach near there and wondered about the suction that had grabbed at my feet. When I told an Alaskan colleague about it, he'd asked, "Didn't you see the signs? That stuff's like quicksand – you might not have come out."

"Signs? I didn't see any signs...."

He told me Turnagain Arm has one of the largest tidal ranges in North America. "When the tide goes out it exposes four miles of mudflats. They're unstable – made of glacial silt. Some people have been trapped in the mud and drowned by incoming tides."

75

When I passed the beach this time on the way to the Bird House bar, I decided to look for the signs I had heard about. Pulling over, I stared across the mudflats and saw one small warning sign: "Dangerous waters and mudflats." That was it. Nothing about quicksand. Nothing about tides. I figured what Alaskans say is true: "If you aren't smart enough to know where you are, you shouldn't be there."

I got back in the car and headed toward Bird Creek. The Bird House bar sat by itself. It looked like a large birdhouse, with faded brown cedar shakes and a big blue bird attached to the front under the eaves. About ten feet high, the bird seemed to be made of papier-mache. I wondered how it held together during the winter. But I knew the place – and the bird – had been there for decades.

I pulled into the parking lot and got out of the car. Above the door, under the bird, was the biggest brassiere I'd ever seen. This should be interesting, I thought.

The building perched at an angle, one end higher than the other. My Seattle friend had told me the 1964 Good Friday earthquake had tilted the bar and everything in it. The owners couldn't afford repairs and just left it the way it was.

Inside, the lighting was dim. I stood near the entrance to get my bearings. Though I could see a few tables, a horseshoe-shaped bar filled most of the room. The floor, covered in sawdust, sloped just like the building. Tree stumps that served as bar stools were slanted as well, and customers held onto their drinks to keep them from sliding into their laps.

Three men in grubby parkas played cards at a table, and four more sat at the bar. Two of them, in their twenties, were deep in conversation.

I sat on a tilted stump, ordered a beer, and asked the bartender how far it was to Portage Glacier.

"About twenty miles south. You going out there now?" he asked.

"Yeah," I said. He seemed to take in my outfit – blouse, thin slacks, flats – but didn't say anything.

I glanced around. The lone window had no glass, but the breeze was offset by a small woodstove in the corner. A pair of deer antlers dangled from a light fixture. The ceiling and walls were covered with bras and panties, pictures and business cards.

"Where'd all those things come from?" I asked the bartender.

"Oh, I don't know, people like to leave stuff behind. And the girls...well, if they take off their panties, they drink free."

The men at the bar glanced up to see my reaction. I tried to look unimpressed. One of the twenty-year-olds, a stocky blond, asked me where I was from.

"Seattle," I said.

He spoke in a low voice to his friend, who mumbled something and shrugged.

Turning to me, he said, "I'm wondering...is it easy to meet women in Seattle? Are the odds better than here?"

"Hmm.... I'm told we have more women. Not sure they're easy to meet."

"Is that right?" he said, thinking it over. "Jack here is having a hard time. I got a girlfriend but he's still looking – a friend of my sister's is coming to meet him tonight." Jack looked embarrassed. He was attractive, well built, and unlike the others, wore a clean shirt and had well-brushed hair.

I would have chatted more with the guys but I tore myself away, aiming to see the glacier before dark.

"Hope it works out," I said, grabbing my jacket and paying for my beer. "Maybe I'll see you later." I left the bar and walked past the bird to my car.

As I drove the next twenty miles, dark clouds appeared in the sky. Following the turnoff for Portage Bay, I took a narrow road to the Visitors Center. A small poster on the door said "Tours, 10 a.m. – 3 p.m. daily." It was four o'clock and the center was closed. The face of the glacier loomed on my right, and I took a rocky path leading in that direction. Within a hundred yards I was walking on ice.

Half a mile later I gazed up at the bluish white ice, longing to see sunlight glinting off the surface. But it was still cloudy. The wind had kicked up and cold air shot through my flimsy jacket. My feet felt like the ice I was walking on. I turned and started back, trying to be quick but aware that I'd be on my own if I fell and got injured.

Halfway back to the path it started raining. "Geez," I said to myself, walking faster. "It's the mudflats all over again." Before I reached the parking lot I was soaked through and could barely feel my hands through my gloves. I got in the car, started the engine and found out the heater was broken. "That's what I get for renting a wreck," I thought. Shaking violently, I drove as fast as I could to the Bird House, got out, ran into the bar and peeled off my dripping wet jacket.

The bartender took one look at me and grabbed the coffee pot. He asked what liquor I wanted in it.

"Anything," I said, sliding onto a barstool.

"Well, here's the coffee." He put down a mug. I savored the sensation of hot liquid pouring down my throat.

The two young men I'd talked with before were at a table in the corner. They were sitting alone, looking glum.

"How'd it go with the girls?" I asked.

The guy with the sister shook his head. "They didn't show."

"Oh that's too bad, I'm sorry," I said.

The bartender came over with a shot glass. "Here, slug this down or mix it in your coffee."

The liquor was perfectly layered: one beige stripe, one brown and one golden.

I heard snickering at the end of the bar. "What's in it?" I asked warily.

"Let's see, Bailey's, Kahlua.... It's called...."

"Oh, I know," I said. "A Screaming Orgasm." The words came out just as he said "a Blow Job."

"What?" I said. The guys at the bar were just as surprised as I was.

The bartender spoke: "Depends on your point of view, I guess."

Somebody at the bar told me to put my mouth on the shot glass and toss it down without using my hands. But I wasn't playing that game. I poured the liquor in my coffee and walked across the room, ready with advice for the lovelorn.

Louisiana

Swamp Special

ONE OF THE BEST MEALS I EVER HAD was on the edge of a swamp at a place called Jimmy's.

After a conference in New Orleans, I was ready for an adventure. Jumping in my rental car, I headed for Honey Island Swamp to find a guy I'd heard of who could take me out on a boat.

Following a friend's directions, I drove north across Lake Pontchartrain, then down an unpaved road until I saw a sign that said "Gator Meat." Pulling over, I walked toward a dock where a man in a twelve-foot skiff looked into a motor. I asked him about a swamp tour.

"This is it," he said. "Name's Tom. Hop right in." He looked amused; I was dressed for a conference, not a boat ride, and must have looked ridiculous in my short skirt, nylons and heels. But he closed the lid on the motor and helped me into the skiff.

We putt-putted through miles of stagnant, murky water while he told me about wildlife in the bayou. He said we were on a marshy arm of the Pearl River, home to hundreds of species of birds, fish and reptiles. Just then a pair of twelve-foot, grey-green alligators slid into the muddy water. They were hard to see except for their bulging eyes.

"Them 'gators eat fish and birds, mostly," he said, "though small mammals get taken, even deer and the occasional bear." I wondered what would happen if the motor conked out. Would they have us for dinner?

The swamp was hot and steamy, drenched in misty sunlight and a dozen shades of green. Spanish moss hung from oaks and Cyprus trees along the shore. Tom switched off the motor and we drifted through reeds and lily pads, the quiet disturbed only by croaking frogs, birdcalls and fish splashing. I relaxed and stopped worrying about the boat and the 'gators. Even the insects left us alone.

After an hour or so Tom turned on the engine and motored back to shore.

I hopped out and strolled toward my car, carrying my shoes. Then I noticed a windowless, faded green building under a willow tree. A sign on the door said "Jimmy's Bar & Grill."

I walked over and peeked my head in the door, blinking as my eyes got used to the darkness. A black Formica bar with eight stools ran down one side of the long, narrow room. Several people sat at small wooden tables, drinking beer and looking at menus. The air smelled of smoke and stale beer.

I hesitated. New Orleans, with its famous Cajun cuisine, was calling. But something told me to try this place. I walked in and took a seat at the counter.

A reed-thin guy with a five o'clock shadow was drying glasses at the other end of the bar. He sauntered over and asked what I wanted.

"I'm not sure," I said. "What's the best thing you have?"

"That would be the special. Crayfish, catfish, grits and alligator."

It sounded like a dare.

The smell of grilling fish made me hungry. I had never tasted alligator but was willing to give it a try. "I'll have it," I said. "And a Dixie beer."

He grabbed one, popped the top off, and took my order to the kitchen. I drank my beer and listened to blues playing softly on the radio. Other diners, mostly men, talked quietly among themselves, except for a couple of guys in the corner celebrating the day's catch. Regulars came in and out, stopping to chat with one another.

Before long the bartender brought me a large oval platter overflowing with food. Half a dozen beady-eyed crayfish stared at a slab of catfish. A pile of grits sat on the side. Overlapping everything was a chunk of alligator tail the length of a small frying pan.

I tried the alligator first. Surprisingly tender and juicy, the meat was barely breaded and lightly fried in oil; it reminded me of veal or frogs' legs. Next I speared a crayfish, seasoned perfectly with cayenne and garlic. The grits were firm and buttery, and lemon brought out the fine flavor of the catfish.

The freshly caught seafood, cooked simply to bring out its natural flavors, made the meal extraordinary. And the humble setting, with its low lighting, good music and pleasant company, enhanced the experience.

I finished every bite. The bartender had been watching me, and I lifted my bottle in a salute. His eyes twinkled and his lean face broke open in a wide, gap-toothed smile.

Missouri

Salad Man

Anne and I were in Kansas City seeking comfort food at the Majestic Steakhouse. We were about to go in when a waiter stuck his head out the door.

"Sorry, ladies, we're done for the night. Only place you'll find supper now is the Phoenix, 8th and Central. Jazz bar, but the food's pretty good."

"Thanks," I said, smiling weakly.

Work had taken me from Seattle to Kansas City and Anne had flown in from Atlanta. We'd been friends since high school and made a point of meeting somewhere once a year. This time my flight had been late and we were looking for dinner at ten o'clock.

We drove to the Garment District and saw a pink neon sign: Phoenix Piano Bar and Grill. Rushing inside, I asked if they were still serving food. "Sure are," said a waiter. "You can sit anywhere."

We sank down into a couple of chairs, relieved. Anne ordered a bottle of wine and started rehashing our high school reunion.

"I can't believe Ben was there," she said. "Did you see his wife?

Elegant woman."

"I know, and Joe Moretti sure looked good. Does he dye his hair?"

"Maybe," said Anne, grinning. "Just like us."

"Was that his girlfriend? She's so young, and that outfit...."

A man slipped in and placed himself on a stool nearby. He was dressed head to toe in black, from his cowboy hat to the embossed leather boots he propped up on the rung of a chair. His salt-and-pepper hair was pulled back in a pony tail, accenting the angles of his face.

"Look at him," I said.

"Wow," replied Anne. "If I were single and ten years younger...."

We saw the guy speak to a waitress, who quickly brought him a salad and a glass of wine. "Did you see that?" I whispered. "A salad! And he's drinking white wine!"

"Omigod, maybe our cowboy's a vegetarian," Anne said. We laughed and went back to our gossip.

Suddenly we heard a voice: "Excuse me, ladies." The dude in black had leaned down from his perch.

"Thought I'd better let you know, they stop serving food at eleven."

"Oh, wow, thanks," I said. Flagging down a waitress, we ordered strip steaks and kept on talking. Salad Man closed his eyes and nodded in time with the music.

"You know, he reminds me of Jimmy Perkins," I said, referring to a guy who'd gone to our high school. "That is, if Jim had acquired a fashion sense."

"True," Anne agreed. "Did I tell you he met me for a drink at the Ritz wearing flip-flops?"

"No!" I laughed and poured another glass of wine.

The cowboy left his seat and headed for the door. He paused between us, bowed slightly and touched our shoulders. "Good night, ladies."

We smiled at him, then looked at each other wide-eyed as he walked away.

"Wow…classy," said Anne.

"Respectful of his elders, perhaps?" I said. My friend glared at me, then laughed.

We turned our attention to the piano guy, who played wildly, pounding the keys as he bounced up and down and shook his long curly hair. When the combo finished it was almost one o'clock. I waved at our waitress and made a signing gesture in the air. She walked over.

"Can you bring our check?" I asked.

"Oh, it's all set. The gentleman sitting over there paid your bill." She pointed to Salad Man's seat.

We sat dumbstruck. Looked at each other. "But who was…"

"…that masked man?" Anne finished.

"No idea – I've never seen him before," the waitress said. All three of us started to giggle. "What a guy," I said.

My friend and I talked about Salad Man all weekend. Anne was determined to figure it out. "Why would he do that out of the blue?" she asked. "We weren't flirting with him."

"Maybe he liked seeing us enjoy ourselves," I said. "Doesn't seem that strange to me."

She mulled it over. "Well, I'll tell you one thing he'll get out of it."

"What?"

"Neither one of us will ever forget him."

Section

5

Retired and Exploring the Galaxy

From our first trip together in the early 1970s, Ron and I were up for a lifetime of travel. We chose to retire in our fifties, hoping to roam as much as possible while we were active and healthy.

To help make that happen, we traded our Craftsman bungalow for a less expensive townhouse. But when we got close to moving, I balked.

"I'm not sure I can do it," I said. "Daniel grew up in this house. I'll miss our clawfoot tub, the French doors, our wood-burning fireplace...."

"Well, I've done the math," Ron said. "If we downsize we can go to Europe every year."

"Oh, OK, then," I said without a pause. "Bye, bye, bungalow." We moved into our townhouse and traveled more than ever.

Six years later an economic downturn hit. Ron tried part-time teaching to refill our coffers and was reminded how much he liked working with special education children. Now his income pays for most of our travel, while I do trip research to maximize those dollars.

Ron and I stretch our funds by traveling off-season, staying in modest, locally-run lodging and choosing low-cost destinations. We visited Eastern Europe to save money, then fell in love with Sarajevo and returned several times.

As senior travelers we can stay longer in a place and rent a small apartment to keep food costs down. We feel more like locals than tourists, shopping daily at the bakery and green-grocer and getting to know our neighbors. We explore nearby towns, find hiking trails or a beach, or just let the day unfold, then come home to relax at the end of the day.

Ron and I enjoy new experiences and meeting people wherever we go. We haven't decided what's next. Maybe we'll follow the Music Trail through the Blue Ridge Mountains. Ride a mailboat along the coast of Norway. Go on safari in Kenya.

Or catch a rocket to another galaxy.

Italy

Il Papa

In 2005 Ron and I traveled to Italy and spent a week in medieval Trevi. The tiny town, perched on a hilltop in Umbria, sat quietly inside its walls, with dramatic views but little else to attract the casual tourist.

Soon after we arrived, I strolled down cobblestone streets, looking for a place to check email. The sun cast a warm glow on aged limestone buildings.

I approached a group of men sitting in the town square. "*Scusi, signori. Dove e un Internet?*" I asked, arms outstretched, typing in the air. One man pointed to the north end of the village. I walked that way but couldn't find an Internet cafe.

I poked my head into a little coffee shop and repeated my question. A dashing, dark-haired barista waved his arms and spoke rapid Italian. When he saw my blank look he stopped mid-word.

"Alberto," he called.

An adolescent appeared from the kitchen and took instructions. The boy motioned for me to follow, then shot down the street and pointed triumphantly to a place called Planet Fun. I peered inside and saw only videogames, but smiled at the boy and said "*Grazie.*"

I went in and ran into a wall of noise. Shouts from a pack of school children competed with a dozen loud machines. The room had no windows and the only light came from the games, whose bright consoles looked like spaceships. I was torn between wanting a computer and hoping not to find one – how could I concentrate in there?

Making my way through the gauntlet of kids, I saw several outdated PCs against the back wall. Nearby a few older men were hunched over a bar. They glanced my way and went back to their conversation. Typical Italians, I thought. No outsiders, especially no women, allowed.

"Lucio!" called one, and another man emerged. His plump face broke into a grin.

"*Buon giorno!*" he said, escorting me to a computer. "*Il costo e tre euro all 'ora.*" About three bucks an hour was fine with me. I did a little work and went home, determined to find my earplugs before returning the next day.

Ron and I had rented a cozy apartment in an eighteenth-century building. Every day we visited a different hill town and returned to Trevi laden with fresh pasta, cheese and vegetables for dinner. Soon the aroma of freshly made pesto tortellini or spaghetti carbonara would fill our apartment, and we'd pass the locally made wine.

At night I'd wander over to Planet Fun. The Italian men ignored me as I emailed and surfed the web. The rapid decline of Pope John Paul II dominated the news, and Italy seemed to be holding its breath. Daily masses were being held throughout the country so Catholics could pray for their beloved Pope.

One day we were out of radio range and missed the BBC News. Back in Trevi, I went to the Internet café. Planet Fun was eerily quiet; games had been turned off and the kids banished. Regulars were on a couch or standing, staring at a TV that hadn't been there before. No one said a word.

As I walked toward them, the owner turned and said, "*Il Papa....*" His face was ashen, the picture of worry and sorrow, as he extended his arm toward the television. Even I could tell the end was near.

Not wanting to intrude, I turned to walk away. But Lucio intercepted me and led me to a computer in the corner. I started reading the news and the men forgot I was there.

Suddenly the first notes of a requiem poured out of the television, signaling the Pope was dead. The men, as one, put their heads in their hands and wept.

When I turned to look at the broadcast, the depth of my feelings surprised me. I thought of Pope John Paul's impact on Italy, Poland and the rest of the world as he fought for the rights of the powerless. And for Italians it was personal. The Pope had been like a father to them while serving as their holy leader for twenty-seven years. I felt humble and filled with compassion. Did I have something in common with these men after all?

Walking softly toward the group, I saw that Lucio seemed like an old man, his body stooped, his face collapsed.

I placed my hands on my heart, then extended them toward him and the others. They seemed grateful for my wordless gesture. Lucio nodded and, with tears streaming down his face, said "*Il Papa li amava tutti....*" He loved us all.

Germany

Finding Franz

A MAN WALKED IN AND MY JAW HIT THE FLOOR. I'd never seen the man before. It was my husband.

Ron and I had traveled to Konstanz, Germany, just north of Switzerland on the banks of the Rhine and the Bodensee (Lake Constance).

Ron was on the trail of his ancestors. As soon as we arrived he disappeared into the city's Archives Office while I set off to explore ancient buildings and tangled passageways. I stopped for coffee on a sunlit square, chatted with locals, and studied the carved wooden doors of a Catholic church. From time to time I pictured Ron holed up in a dark, dusty cellar, surrounded by cobwebs and ancestral records.

I had become a genealogy widow. Back home Ron had spent hours on the computer, building family charts and making breathless announcements: "My grandmother's great, great grandfather was born in Massachusetts in 1805, and his mother came from England in 1790, but his father was a teacher in...." My eyes would glaze over and I'd mutter, "Whatever...just don't quiz me on it."

But I was happy to be in Konstanz. When Ron eventually caught up with me I was sitting by the lake, enjoying a glass of chilled Riesling.

"There you are," he said, barely able to contain himself.

"Oh, hi. Have a sip of wine, it's delicious. Do you know that's Switzerland over there? Konstanz is so close to the Swiss border they didn't bomb it during World War II. Isn't that....?"

"Wait, wait, you won't believe this. I found out where the Schwerts are buried – in Binningen, only twenty miles from here."

"That's nice," I said.

The next morning we took off in the rain, looking for Ron's ancestral village among rolling hills and farmland. After a few wrong turns we found Binningen and the Roman Catholic Church. Ron leapt out and made a beeline for the cemetery, while I stayed warm and dry in the car. He returned a half hour later to report he'd spotted five Schwert graves.

"You're soaked to the skin," I exclaimed. "Was it worth it?"

"Oh, yeah," he said, grinning from ear to ear. I shook my head as he climbed into the car and we headed back to Konstanz.

On the way out of town I spotted a gasthaus, the only sign of life in the tiny village. It was getting late; Ron hesitated, but I thought we should stop and celebrate his discoveries.

The pub was brightly lit, with beige paneled walls and white linoleum floors. Pungent odors of sauerbraten and red cabbage drifted out from the kitchen. Half a dozen men sat drinking beer and speaking quietly in German. When we plunked down beside them, their conversation ceased.

Sylvia, our waitress, came to the table. We ordered beers, and she asked us if that was all.

"Well," said Ron, "I'm looking for information about the Schwert family." He used the German pronunciation, "Schvairt."

"Do you know any....?"

Pub owner Jesse, who had emerged from the kitchen, overheard our query. She and Sylvia questioned the men in German. They came alive, exchanging information and nodding emphatically. Sylvia turned to Ron. "They say you look like a Schvairt."

"I do?" Ron asked, astonished.

Jesse spoke into her cell phone. Then she announced, "Don't worry, he's coming over."

"Who?" Ron said.

"Franz Schwert."

We looked at each other, speechless. I thought Ron was going to burst.

"*D-Danke schoen*," he managed.

Less than ten minutes later, Franz walked through the door. He was Ron's *doppelganger*, from his height and build to their common facial features. He walked straight to my husband, shook his hand and clasped his shoulder.

"I didn't know I had relatives in America."

Franz placed a family chart on the table next to Ron's. They matched perfectly until the point when Sigmund Schwert, Ron's great grandfather, had emigrated to the United States. Ron and Franz realized they had the same great, great grandfather.

I was delighted for the men and amazed at the power of genetics. Here were third cousins who could have been brothers, sitting at the table with their identical profiles bent at the same angle over their charts. Even their eyeglasses were alike. And they shared a passion for genealogy, which was rubbing off on me.

The pub regulars looked at Ron, then Franz, then Ron again.

They sent us a message through Sylvia: "We are happy to be here at this historic moment." Their faces, so dour when we arrived, were beaming.

Franz took us home to meet the family. His wife Ursula greeted us with open arms, and their twenty-year-old daughter Sabina translated for her mother and brother Clements. Sitting in their cozy kitchen, we shared stories of lives lived more than a continent apart.

Due in Munich the next day, we reluctantly said goodbye after dinner. They urged us to return and we invited them to Seattle. When I got to our car, Ursula rushed over and put her arm around my shoulders, squeezing me tight. I understood: now that we'd found each other, it was hard to let go.

As we drove back to Konstanz, Ron and I felt euphoric and sad. "I wish my parents were alive," said my husband, emotion tugging at his lips. "Wouldn't they have loved this?"

"No doubt," I replied. "Just as I did." A name on a document had come to life, and I finally understood the magic of genealogy.

Munich Redux

As our train approached Munich and farmland gave way to clusters of neat houses and tall apartment buildings, my thoughts went back to a trip there thirty years earlier. Ron and I had drunk too much in crowded beer halls, eaten cheap food and slept in a tiny backpacker's tent. It was fun when we were young, but I wanted a little more comfort this time.

We checked into Munich's Easy Palace hostel and went for a stroll on the pedestrian mall. A slim, dark-haired beauty played a flute in the town square, filling the block with music. At a nearby *bierstube*, a friendly waitress with blond braids served us cabbage rolls and spaetzle. Nourished and relaxed, we returned to the Easy Palace for a good night's sleep.

At noon the next day, a crowd gathered at Town Hall to gaze up at a giant clock, the famous Rathaus-Glockenspiel. Chimes echoed through the square. Life-size figures popped out of the clock and took part in a noble wedding, followed by knights jousting on horseback. When it was over, we walked on in search of the Saturday market.

A farmer in *lederhosen* stood at the entrance with several animals. Every few minutes his rooster would drink water from a bottle, or his collie would dance on two legs. When a passerby dropped a coin in a box, a duck quacked what sounded like "thank you."

We walked into the market and saw a man, dressed as a large bee, selling honey. Feelers sprang from his yellow, frizzy wig, and daffodil-colored tights stuck out of his padded, black-and-yellow-striped body suit. After taking his picture, I moved from stall to stall. Homemade pastries, crafts, local cheese and produce were all artfully displayed.

Ron had followed his nose to a food stand and came rushing over to get me. Soon we were standing at a high table with several Germans, eating bratwurst and sauerkraut. As I lifted my beer stein, part of my sausage slipped to the ground, followed by "thump-thump-thump-slurp." A small terrier, his tiny leg in a cast, had hobbled over and quickly grabbed the meat. Everyone at our table burst out laughing.

That evening, despite my newfound delight in Munich, I couldn't face the Hofbrauhaus and its mobs of tourists. The guidebook referred us to Jodlerwirt, a small, "smart-alecky" pub. I wondered what that meant and hoped it wasn't too young and hip for us.

We found the bar on a quiet street, away from the revelry in the town square. When we walked into a quiet cocktail lounge, I remembered the book's advice: "Don't stay downstairs. The party is on the second floor."

We climbed a set of small, winding steps and opened a door. Noise poured out into the hallway. Inside the brightly lit room, two accordion players dressed in traditional white shirts, red suspenders and lederhosen tapped their well-shined shoes. The musicians beamed as the crowd sang, swayed and hoisted their beers. Right away I felt glad to be there.

We sat at one of the picnic tables filling the room. Everyone spoke German, but the patrons were friendly and we could follow the action. Two old ladies in flowered dresses leaned toward each other, whispering. Children stayed seated and laughed with their parents, while a busty young woman flirted with a waiter.

Soon a young man arrived and sat down beside me. He wore tight-waisted trousers and a blousy white shirt that set off his startling blue eyes and spiked blond hair. A waiter brought him a beer, and he drew two long wooden spoons out of his knapsack.

When the accordions started up again, Spoon Man went into action. His utensils flew around him, front and back, in wild percussion. With increasing velocity he played the spoons on his knees and arms, on nearby tables, and on the rears of a few customers. For his encore he wielded a scrub brush and broom with equal enthusiasm, rapping the handles on every hard surface. Everyone cheered.

Just when I thought the place couldn't get any better, five young men arrived, slid onto our bench and introduced themselves. With English-speaking Helmut now sitting beside me, I could finally have a conversation.

Helmut's eager face was bright and engaged as he leaned in to make himself heard. "Where are you from?" he asked.

"Seattle, in the U.S., the northwest cor...." I said.

"I know, I know just where it is. Near Vancouver, right?" He nodded furiously and beamed. "Have you been in Germany long?"

"Oh, about two we...."

"You like it?"

"We love it; Munich is so...."

"*Ja*, we have a great time always here."

I wedged in a question. "You and your friends? Are you here for work?"

"No, no, we get away once a year, to play some poker. Our wives stay home in northern Germany with the babies."

I was starting to understand their jubilant mood.

"What does your husband do in the States?" continued Helmut.

"Ron is a teacher and I work at a university."

"How about that!" he said with amazement, jumping up and down in his seat. "My friend is a teacher too! Juergen," he yelled, pointing in our direction. "This man is a teacher in the States!"

Juergen smiled and gave a "thumbs up" to Ron, who nodded back.

"The rest of us work for companies, just jobs, you know. Someday we retire too, and get to travel all the time." He waved at a waiter, and five beers magically appeared. Helmut clinked our glasses and yelled *"Jawohl!"*

"Do you drink beer in the States?" he asked. "We always drink beer, except for a Schnapps. What do you drink?"

"Well, let's see," I said, "Irish whiskey, and..."

His head reared back, eyes like saucers. "Irish VISKEY?"

"Yeah, and Ron likes vodka..."

Head further back, eyes wider. "WODKA?" he shrieked. Ron rocked with laughter and the group burst into song.

A few hours later we bade goodbye to our new German friends and took our leave of the Jodlerwirt. Outside, the moon was full and the city quiet; only a few people strolled across the majestic town square. Looking up, I saw gables and cornices lit up against the night sky.

I was glad I hadn't given up on the city. With a little planning, our trip had gone smoothly, and connecting with people made me fall in love with Munich.

Ireland

The Old Mariner

I was tucked into a window seat at a café with a cup
of coffee, looking down on a small harbor in Bunbeg, Ireland.
Two sailboats and a trawler bobbed gently in the calm water.
The sun came and went on a cool spring day.

A beige Ford sedan pulled up next to a boat ramp and an
old man stepped out. Stocky, with thin, white hair, he wore
a maroon sweater vest and tie, a wind jacket and a tweed
fisherman's cap.

The dapper gent walked haltingly to a rowboat at the top of the
ramp and removed a padlock. He went back to his car, put on a
life jacket, took out two oars and carried them to the boat. Then
he went back and let out a small mutt, who limped toward the
ramp. The man picked him up and placed him in the stern.

I wondered how he'd get his craft to the water. Then I noticed
two handles jutting from the back of the dinghy and a wheel
attached to the bow. The man lifted the handles and pushed
the boat down the ramp like a wheelbarrow.

When the bow was afloat, he stepped in and pushed off.
The old gent rowed steadily across the harbor and out the
mouth of the Clady River. I wondered where he was going,
then realized he must be making a circle and would come

back to the dock and his ride home. An old sailor's version of a daily constitutional.

Spain

Holy Week in Sevilla

"THRUMP, THRUMP," BEAT THE DRUMS, followed by trumpets blaring. A parade! I thought. But where was it?

A group of people walking ahead of us dashed down an alley and we followed them. Old ladies in flowered dresses hustled arm-in-arm while a girl with ribboned pigtails bounced on her father's shoulders. Youths in black leather hurried to join the crowd.

It was Palm Sunday, and Ron and I were in Sevilla for *Semana Santa* (Holy Week), the most spectacular religious festival in Spain. Starting today, and for seven days before Easter, fifty processions would crisscross the city with a hundred *pasos* (floats, or altars) among them.

We turned into a narrow street packed with hundreds of people. I squeezed in and craned my neck to see the parade.

"Look at that," I gasped. A huge altar was coming toward us, with rows of people marching solemnly before it. A barefoot young man led the way. He wore a flowing white tunic and labored under a six-foot cross. Two priests followed, waving large incense burners over the crowd. Then came dozens of men in long black robes and tall, narrow, cone-shaped hoods. I shivered at the sight of them. "Must be the penitents," said Ron. Each year, thousands of Catholics offer penance for their sins by covering their faces and marching in parades.

Following the marchers was an altar with a life-size statue of Jesus riding a donkey. The platform it sat on was the size of a small bedroom, yet seemed to float above the street. I wondered how it stayed up.

Suddenly a slim man in a beige linen suit appeared, yelling as he ran alongside the paso: "*Ir a la derecha, un poco más, buena, adelante, un poco a la izquierda*" ("Go right, a little more, good, forward, a little to the left"). I realized the altar was being carried by people underneath it, who needed directions since they couldn't see where they were going.

The heavy, gilded float missed us by inches as it headed down the narrow street, its statues tilting precariously. Onlookers leaned over their balconies and cheered as the figures sailed by.

"Unbelievable," I said, shaking my head as we walked away. "I had no idea…." Not usually drawn to religious events, I was excited about this one.

"I know," said Ron. "What a spectacle."

"We need a parade schedule," I said. "I don't want to miss anything."

Little did I know the processions would continue around the clock all over the city. My official Holy Week program showed parade routes and schedules day by day, using different colored lines like a city transit map. Processions lasted from six to fourteen hours, and ended up at La Giralda, the largest Gothic cathedral in the world.

Our cozy apartment in historic Barrio Santa Cruz was a welcome refuge during the nonstop festival. That evening, Ron and I found a tapas bar in our neighborhood with seating outside. We sipped wine and dined on grilled sea bass as an old man drifted among the tables playing a concertina. Women in flowing skirts and men in shiny jackets sauntered by, enjoying their *paseo*, or nightly stroll.

After supper we walked through Maria Luisa Park and saw families gathered for Holy Week. Elderly matrons held court with their children and grandchildren. A young mother cradled a pink-flanneled infant while her husband played with their little boys. Ron and I sat quietly on a bench, watching the sun go down.

Half an hour later we heard trumpets coming from the Plaza de España and ran to watch another parade. Drums led the way for penitents draped in white with purple hoods. In the dark, the pageant looked more mysterious than the first one we had seen. The highlight was a covered float carrying the Virgin of the Brotherhood of San Roque.

"There she is," I said to Ron, gazing upward. "Oh my god."

Under her fragile canopy, the life-size Virgin wore a dark green mantle, her face glowing in the light of a hundred candles. I could see her dark eyes and lashes, the blush on her cheeks.

Slowly the altar moved forward, trembling in the soft night breeze. One candle went out and the procession stopped. An elderly man who walked next to the float propped a primitive wooden ladder against the structure and climbed slowly to the top. He lit the candle, and then eased back down again. The *costaleros* – penitents who carry the floats – must have been resting under the paso. Three claps rang out; they lifted the platform and lunged forward as the music swelled and the crowd roared.

Ron and I followed the parade. Onlookers gasped when the Virgin came into view, then cheered as she passed by.

I'd read that each of Sevilla's fifty parishes has its own procession. Church brotherhoods founded hundreds of years ago sponsor the floats. Traditions have been handed down from generation to generation: fathers take their infants to view the dazzling altars, and these early impressions stay with them to be shared with their own children.

Most families give endless hours to the event. Girls work hard to earn the honor of sewing garments for the Virgin, and young men train for years to be *costaleros* during Holy Week. As thousands of the faithful create the rich, complex celebration, Semana Santa becomes a communal experience for 100,000 people.

Sevillanos worship the Virgin Mary all year, not only in church but during their everyday lives. Her image appears in *azulejos*, tiles found on the walls of bars and restaurants, homes and workplaces, where believers can pause and pray to her. That night she came alive, as she had every year for centuries. The pageant moved me in ways I couldn't understand.

Ron and I went back to Barrio Santa Cruz and partied late into the night. That was Sevilla during Holy Week: solemn, candle-lit processions near restaurants filled with revelers; spectators crying, then shouting with joy. The contrasts arose from the belief that Jesus' suffering brought hope to the world. As a booklet about Holy Week says, Semana Santa celebrates "heartache and love, the flesh and the spirit, the dead and the living; they are all in the street."

As the week progressed, more people flooded the city. I could feel excitement build in anticipation of Good Friday's processions, whose pasos would display the holiest symbols of Semana Santa.

They began on Thursday at midnight. Several hours beforehand we nabbed a tiny table outside a café on the parade route. Ron ordered a bottle of Barbadillo in a champagne bucket filled with ice. We made it last all night, waiting with thousands of others while the pageant crawled through the city.

Finally a giant altar came into view. Hundreds of marchers surrounded a three-ton float depicting *Jesús del Gran Poder* (Jesus of the Great Power). Draped in a heavy robe embroidered with gold, Jesus bowed his head and looked resigned as a man read his death sentence. For fourteen hours, forty-eight men would carry the paso on their shoulders in forty-five-minute shifts. Dozens of musicians followed the float, playing a slow dirge with bugles and drums.

Then came another float holding *La Esperanza Macarena,* the Weeping Virgin, under a velvet canopy embroidered in gold. Her delicate face had deep-set, shadowed eyes. Crystal tears of sorrow ran down her cheeks.

Spectators leaned over balconies, wept and threw roses; the depth of their love for Macarena was clear. As a Spaniard once said, "She knows all the problems of Sevilla and its people. We've been confiding in her for centuries. To us, she is hope. That's her name: Esperanza."

Once the Good Friday parades had passed by, everyone disbursed quietly. It was five a.m.

I'd been warned that I could never prepare myself for the full impact of Holy Week in Sevilla. In the end I was deeply moved by the religious devotion of the people, centuries of shared history, and the cultural achievement that was Semana Santa.

Two days after the last procession, Easter arrived with a burst of unrestrained joy. Bells rang from dozens of churches and people poured out after Mass, their faces radiant as they greeted one another. Afterward they went home for family celebrations. Throughout the year Sevillanos would practice their religion at home and in church. We had joined them briefly, celebrating in the streets, but we'd no longer share that part of their lives.

Ron and I stayed for another week. We wandered down empty streets, past quiet restaurants, hearing women making dinner and calling to their children. The people of Sevilla had returned to their normal lives and their constant faith.

Spain

Springtime in Segovia

FROM A HILLTOP IN SEGOVIA'S OLD CITY, Ron and I watched sleek black birds dive through the arches of a Roman aqueduct.

"Why do they do it?" I wondered aloud.

"Wouldn't you if you could?" Ron replied.

Segovia, about sixty miles northwest of Madrid, is known for its stunning Gothic Cathedral and its first-century aqueduct, an engineering masterpiece. We arrived on a warm spring day. Sun peeked out of the clouds and the scent of almond blossoms filled the air. Locals and tourists wandered through the city, talking and laughing.

Free entertainment appeared like magic around every corner. On leafy Plaza Mayor, a man in a zoot suit played a piano while a small crowd danced and clapped to the music. Not far away, a dozen children rode finely-carved, gilded unicorns on a 100-year-old carousel.

In a tiny square tucked among eighteenth-century buildings, we saw a three-foot-tall wooden puppet dancing to recorded music. His red shoes tapped across a platform as he waved his arms, urging his puppet pals to join him.

A man pulled the strings that brought the puppets to life. With a lined face and long white hair that flew around him when he moved, he looked like a character from an old story book. He stomped behind his lively marionettes and spoke their lines, but everyone forgot he was there. Adults and children alike seemed enthralled. As the story came to a close, the puppeteer invited children to climb onstage and march behind the puppets. Everyone sang and cheered.

As we walked away, the sun was setting. Most people had left the old town and Segovia was growing quiet. We strolled along a path in the upper part of the city, gazing down on buildings and meadows bathed in orange light.

We turned a corner and came across a tall, slim man wearing a grey batik cape and billowing black pants. He stood on a terrace holding a saxophone and had an open box in front of him. Just behind him sat a small, scruffy Papillon – a type of toy spaniel. He was black and white with long hair and fringed ears.

I threw a half-euro into the box. The man raised his horn and started to play. At the same time the little dog moved forward, pointed his muzzle to the sky and howled softly, matching the mellow sound of the saxophone. After a few minutes the man stopped playing; he handed a biscuit to the pup, who went quietly back to his spot. Then Ron threw in a euro; the man played again, and the dog stepped up and sang. A dozen people had gathered to watch.

Unseen by the Papillon, a fluffy white poodle with a girlie-pink collar stood in the back of the small crowd, craning her neck to see what was going on. When she and her owner moved on, they walked past the singing dog, who stopped mid-note. Eyes bugged out, he looked at his master, looked back at the poodle, and shot after her down the street.

The saxman shrugged, smiled and finished his song.

Ukraine

Monkey on My Back

"I AM PROUD TO ANNOUNCE THE VISA REQUIREMENT for the United States has been lifted. Welcome to Ukraine!" declared President Viktor Yushchenko on the official Ukrainian website.

Ron and I were eager to accept the president's invitation. I wanted to connect with my Ukrainian roots and explore Kiev and Odessa, known for their stunning architecture and rich cultural life.

Both of us had enjoyed traveling in Eastern Europe – dining on Krakow's medieval main square, driving down the Dalmatian Coast, strolling along Ljubljana's River of Seven Names. We'd found the locals generous, kind and curious, eager to discuss history and politics. Even those who didn't speak English tried to be helpful.

But navigating Ukraine was a different story.

Ron and I flew from Budapest to Kiev in May of 2006. As we walked out of the customs area, a scowling man with a shaved head held the only sign with non-Cyrillic letters: "Schwert."

"Urngh," he grunted as we approached. Grabbing our bags, he charged out of the airport – refusing to stop when we pointed to a currency exchange booth – and led us to his car.

In the cab the driver dialed a number and handed me his cell phone. It was someone from the agency that had rented us an apartment. She said our place wasn't ready and we'd have to stay in another one.

"Don't worry," she said. "Ivan knows where it is." She hung up before I could say anything.

Ivan sped into the city and screeched to a halt outside a stark, rundown building. He dumped our backpacks in the hall, gave us a key, pointed up the stairs and left without a word. It was four p.m. on a Friday and Ron and I had no idea where we were.

We moved our bags into the apartment, then ran outside to a bank. The ATM declined our debit card and the teller inside refused to honor travelers checks and credit cards. We traded our small stash of dollars for *hryvnias* and hoped they would last through the weekend.

Ron and I faced more hurdles every time we left our apartment. I couldn't figure out the phone system, and computers at the Internet café had Cyrillic letters. When we tried to get help, people were indifferent or rude.

Then one day we emerged and were amazed at what we saw. Streets had been decorated overnight and brightly dressed revelers filled the old city. A children's parade went by, followed by rollerbladers in matching outfits waving orange flags. Music played everywhere.

It was Kiev Day, which commemorates the founding of Ukraine's capital city. Ron and I joined hundreds of people and soaked up the excitement.

On Independence Square we saw a guy offering pictures with his monkey for five hryvnias (fifty cents) a pop. I paid my money and he put his pet on my shoulder. The monkey was silver grey with white around his neck. His face was small and round, and his black eyes glistened.

"Isn't he cute?" I asked Ron.

The man turned the monkey so his long, curly tail wrapped around my neck. He gave me a broad smile.

"Ah," I thought, "We're finally making a connection."

Just as Ron snapped the photo, I felt warm liquid pour down the back of my neck. The monkey seemed to whisper in my ear, "Welcome to Kiev."

Only later did I notice that all the other monkeys posing for pictures were wearing diapers.

Ukraine

Opening Doors

RON AND I LOVE GOING TO FOREIGN COUNTRIES, meeting challenges and getting to know the people. But Ukraine was different. We could barely take care of basics and weren't connecting with anyone.

Locals refused to make eye contact in our apartment building and on the street. They seemed closed and cautious, even to each other. Perhaps government suppression had taught people not to trust anyone, even their neighbors. The friendships we had made in other places were missing in Ukraine – until I got locked inside a bathroom.

It all started in Odessa when I walked by a performance hall and saw a colorful poster on the wall. I approached the ticket window and held out my wallet. The clerk wrote down forty *hryvni* (five dollars), then pointed to Saturday on the calendar. I held up two fingers and gave her eighty hryvni, figuring we could spend ten dollars to find out what was playing.

"Guess what," I said to Ron when I got back to our apartment. He looked up from his book.

"We're going out Saturday night," I continued.

"For what?" he asked.

"I don't know, but it cost five dollars each. I think it might be a concert."

"Sounds good," he said.

On Saturday I put on the only dress I had with me and Ron wore a tweed jacket. It was a warm, spring evening. We walked to the hall, grabbing a couple of *piroshkis* and beers on the way. Other people, mostly in pairs, gathered outside the drab cement building, the men in dark-colored suits and most of the women wearing long skirts and embroidered blouses. Many sat on a low wall near the sidewalk, eating food they had brought with them. We joined them with our piroshkis, but got no response when we nodded and smiled.

When the theater opened, we walked up the steps and into the building. The lobby was elegant, with a high carved ceiling, chandeliers and thick red carpet. The hum of voices got louder as the lobby filled with people.

I wasn't sure how long the concert would last, so I decided to use the bathroom.

Ron sighed. "Please hurry," he said, planting himself against a lobby wall. He got tired of waiting for me and claimed I always had a new excuse for taking a long time.

I hurried down a lengthy corridor and descended a staircase. Turning right, I went through a door that looked like a bathroom. Inside was a dank, concrete room with a dim light revealing four stalls.

While in one, I heard other ladies come and go, chattering in Ukrainian. Then, when I was ready to leave, the lock wouldn't budge. I jiggled the bolt and pushed the door, sure the situation was temporary. By the time I realized I was stuck, the last woman had left the bathroom.

Mmm...maybe I could crawl under the door, I thought. I visualized what that would do to my pale green dress, and in any case, the space between the floor and the door was less than a foot. Perhaps I'd stand on the toilet and climb over the top. But it was too high to reach. I thought of Ron waiting in the lobby.

"Hellooo," I called from the stall, banging the door with my fist. I yanked the lock back and forth, up and down. Banged some more. The stall seemed like a prison. I was afraid, wondering if Ron had noticed what direction I'd gone in.

Then I heard heels clicking rapidly, getting closer, giving me hope. Two women rushed in and entered the stalls. When I heard a flush, I jiggled the lock and banged the door again, worried they would rush off to the performance. But when the women emerged, they stopped at my door and spoke to each other in Ukrainian.

"What's going on?" one seemed to ask.

The other woman asked me a question, but I couldn't understand.

"Help!" I said plaintively, trying to recall the word for "please."

The lights flashed on and off signaling the start of the concert.

One of the ladies pulled on my door, while the other, in a no-nonsense voice, gave me instructions on what to do. But she was speaking Ukrainian.

A third woman rushed in and used the toilet. She was enlisted, and the three women held a summit on my behalf.

Finally the new person stood close to my door and spoke sharply. Somehow I knew what to do. I pushed the door with all my might at the same time she was pulling. I burst out to find three women in their sixties wearing well-worn dresses; one had on beige-colored silk and the others wore dark blue velvet. We stood there, stunned. Then we all started laughing.

"*Dakuju*," I said, remembering the word for "thank you."

I felt elated to be free and glad I had connected with my rescuers. Who knew that being locked in a bathroom would bring out the best in people?

We lingered for a few moments, smiling and nodding as we washed our hands. Then we all tore out the door and up the stairs. I ran ahead of them to the lobby.

Ron was not amused. "What's your story this time?" he said. The program of music and commentary had started.

"Tell you during intermission," I said, as the other women sailed by with their husbands, all of whom looked just as annoyed as Ron.

The Tiny Red Kettle

"Sarajevo is open for tourists," *The Times of London* reported. Pictures of red roofs and snow-capped mountains leapt off the page. Bosnia had emerged from the 1990s war and rebuilt its infrastructure, but tourists had yet to discover the country. It was time to go.

Ron and I flew from Milan to Sarajevo, full of plans for exploring the city and learning about its history. We had rented an apartment for two weeks and hoped to relax, cook our own meals, and take in the sights without rushing.

We landed on a hot, humid afternoon and took a cab from the airport, through miles of gritty neighborhoods. Beat-up trams clanged along their rails, cars honked and construction dust surrounded our vehicle. I missed Riomaggiore, the ancient village we had left behind, with its narrow lanes and houses tumbling down to the sea. Why did we leave Italy? I wondered, feeling like I'd been plucked from one century and put down in another.

Our taxi driver was in his fifties and looked like James Garner – handsome with thick black hair and a hearty laugh. He bonded quickly with Ron in the front seat, talking as if they were old friends. The guy turned into a tour guide, pointing out sights like an elegant mosque and a garish Holiday Inn where journalists stayed while reporting on the 1990s war. He showed us buildings going up to replace those bombed, saying "*Kaput!*" and smiling broadly each time. Like a New York cabbie, he leaned over and talked nonstop, hardly glancing at the road. I admired his positive attitude but felt too tired and nervous to enjoy the ride.

We rounded a corner and the old town appeared, with its picturesque squares and bridges crossing the Miljacka River. Houses dotted the hillsides surrounding the city, with forests and mountains beyond. Small graveyards tucked among neighborhoods overflowed with narrow headstones from the recent war.

The driver pulled up to our hostel but kept on chatting until a young man appeared and greeted us warmly. He was in his twenties, tall and lean with a dazzling smile. He explained he was the owner's son and showed us to our apartment – or, as Ron would soon call it, our "so-called apartment."

The place was newly remodeled and the sun shone in through a skylight. One area had four single beds while the other had a couch, loveseat and armchair made of dark brown leather. But the apartment had no kitchen – not even a hot plate or mini-fridge. Not a glass, dish or utensil. No cookware. It also lacked towels, soap and hangers. We were dumbfounded, but soon realized the hostel owner's definition of "apartment" was not the same as ours. I had never asked about a kitchen, just assumed we would have one. Even after thirty years of travel, I had things to learn about renting an apartment.

The towels, it turned out, were an oversight; when Ron requested a few, the owner's son smacked himself on the head and delivered them in minutes. Showing off his English, he said, "Tell me if you need anything else, I will help you."

I didn't know where to start. "Perhaps an electric kettle?" I asked.

"We do not have, but...." The young man bolted down the stairs, indicating that we should follow. He showed us the common room, thick with cigarette smoke, and gestured proudly toward a stove and a single saucepan we could use to boil water. I appreciated the gesture but couldn't help thinking of our kitchen in Italy where we had lingered over freshly made coffee while gazing out at the Mediterranean.

Ron and I nodded, smiled and retreated upstairs, where we sat on one of our couches and stared at each other, depressed.

"What's the point of having an apartment if we can't make a cup of tea?" I asked, thinking how much I could use one. I had a sinus infection and could hardly breathe. At least our room wasn't smoky.

"Maybe we should find another place," said Ron.

"I don't know...we just got here; let's give it a chance."

We decided to try and make the apartment work, with a bottom line of being able to make breakfast: coffee, juice and cereal.

Setting out that evening, we headed for Bascarsija, or Pigeon Square, a block from our apartment in the heart of old town. People of all ages strolled along cobblestone streets, chatted and waved to friends. Worshippers went in and out of mosques responding to calls for prayer, peaceful sounds coming from loudspeakers attached to the outside of minarets. Others window-shopped or sat at outside cafes, sipping tea or wine. I was struck by how relaxed they were; Muslim women in simple head scarves mingled with those in miniskirts. Everyone seemed to be enjoying themselves.

One small square looked like an outdoor living room. Rug-covered benches lined the walls of buildings and colorful hassocks dotted the courtyard. Locals drank tea from a nearby cafe, and some smoked tobacco using large, shared hookahs. Children played underneath a tree growing in the center of the square.

We pulled ourselves away from the scene and found a grocery that sold paper plates, napkins and a dishpan, which I figured would double as a refrigerator once I filled it with cold water. Another store had apples and bananas, granola and milk, along with vodka and fresh-squeezed, blood-red orange juice. There, on a high shelf, I saw an ancient, dust-covered container holding two ceramic cups and a pound of coffee; a tall clerk leapt up and got it for me. Now all we needed was a way to boil water, though we were prepared to use hot tap water if necessary.

Late the next day we found another market in a corrugated steel building that looked like a Quonset hut. The cavernous place had twenty-foot ceilings and dozens of stalls, most abandoned and covered by tarps at the end of the day. The place was quiet except for the sound of a few ancient carts being rolled across the bare cement floor.

I lit up when I saw a small red kettle that looked like a measuring cup with a cord. An elderly woman stood nearby wearing a worn peasant skirt and green vest, with a thin beige scarf tied around her head. I wondered if she wore it for religious reasons or simply to keep her hair back.

Gesturing toward the pint-sized plastic pitcher, I raised my eyebrows and smiled. She dug it out quickly and held up five fingers; the item would cost five Bosnian Marks (BAMs), about $3.50. Ron nodded vigorously and paid her. With that he had reached his shopping threshold and told me he'd wait outside.

Next I pointed to a water glass, almost hidden in a different stall. The old lady took a cell phone out of her pocket and made a call, presumably to find out the price. A man drifted over, then a mother and her child. None of the four understood my language, but they all seemed determined to get me what I wanted. Finally the old woman held up four fingers. When I beamed and gave her the money, she handed me a set of three glasses. What a bargain!

Then I noticed hangers holding clothes for sale. I touched one, and the man removed a denim jacket and held it up for me. I shook my head no and tried to show I wanted hangers instead of clothes. Another woman joined the party, and all five people leaned in, trying to understand me. When I pointed at all the hangers, they seemed to think I wanted all the clothes. Finally a light bulb went off in the man's head. "Ah!" he said and dragged over a bin with hangers for sale, five for one BAM. I held up ten fingers, handed over a two-BAM coin and emerged triumphantly to show Ron my prizes.

Breakfast the next morning featured our little red kettle boiling water for coffee. We were all set up for the next two weeks and felt less like tourists than locals, running errands in the neighborhood. I took pride in making the apartment work, but the more I learned about the suffering of Sarajevans during the 1990s war, the more I wondered how we could have been so distressed by such small inconveniences.

One night our hostel owner Salem invited us into his living room for a chat. Like most people we met in Sarajevo, he spoke excellent English. Before long our conversation turned to war, and our host described how the people of Sarajevo survived for almost four years with very little food and no electricity, gas or other services. They walked miles to get water while dodging shells and sniper fire. Yet they defied their Serbian enemies by living as normally as they could. Sarajevans got dressed and went to work, though they weren't getting paid. They fell in love, got married, had babies and held funerals, though many were shot while trying to bury their loved ones. They attended school and cultural events in basements. And throughout the brutal war, they shared all they had with one another.

Sarajevans held onto their spirit and dignity, even their sense of humor; one man told me he'd learned that burning a size forty-three shoe would cook a sausage.

Salem pronounced himself "satisfied with life" because he could turn on a tap and get water. But since their country was considered unstable, Bosnians couldn't get visas; Salem felt sorry for his sons, who wanted to travel and "meet the peoples." Ron and I understood, since travel was so important to us. And isn't that what travel is all about – meeting the peoples of the world?

We fell in love with Sarajevo and kept the little red kettle. When we travel it sustains us – and reminds us of the city's brave survivors.

Croatia

Social Climbers

"LET'S FIND THAT ROOFTOP BAR," Ron said when we arrived in Korcula, on the Croatian island of the same name. The fifteenth-century town had been built in a herringbone pattern that circulated air among buildings and gave protection from strong ocean winds. Ron had read about a place perched on an ancient tower with a 360-degree view of the city and the Adriatic Sea. "If we hurry we can catch the sunset."

I was ready to unpack and settle in, but when Ron flew out the door I was right behind him.

In May the town was quiet, with hardly any tourists. We hurried through the narrow cobblestone streets and emerged from an alley to see a harbor. Sailboats and small cruise ships floated in the sunlit water. We turned right and walked below the old town wall, taking in the view and the scent of sea air.

"Look," said Ron, spotting a sign with a picture of a tower. "C'mon."

We climbed up a staircase outside the tower and entered a small round room with stone walls and one tiny window. Several people sat at tables tucked into nooks around the room. We took more stairs to a second level, where half a dozen men were drinking beer and speaking Croatian.

One of them pointed to a ladder. I walked over, looked up and saw a hole in the ceiling and a circle of blue sky.

The men stopped talking and watched as Ron scampered up the twelve-foot ladder to the roof. I followed, climbing hand-over-hand, with my purse looped over my arm and my coat tied around my waist. Halfway up the ladder, my coat slipped down to my ankles, trapping me so I couldn't go up or down.

Ron peered back through the hole. "C'mon, you can do it," he said. "What's taking you so long?"

Clinging to a rung with one hand, I reached down and grabbed my coat with the other and kept on climbing. When I finally emerged, dragging my coat and purse, the drinkers on the roof looked relieved. Perhaps they had pictured a very old woman struggling up the ladder.

"This is NOT the grand entrance I had pictured," Ron declared.

A ripple of laughter went around the dozen or so people sitting on the roof, bundled up against the wind. Then they went back to conversations in four or five languages.

We sat at an empty table. A waiter came over and took our order, which he clipped to a basket with a clothespin and sent over the wall. Ten minutes later the same basket brought up our cocktails without spilling a drop.

Relaxing with our drinks, we watched others emerge through the hole with expressions of wonder and relief. I tried not to think about going back down the ladder.

A young couple came up, plopped down at our table and introduced themselves as Simon and Naomi from Australia. They were on their way to a family wedding in Scotland and bubbled over with excitement about their trip.

Soon two men popped out of the hole. The Australians invited them to join us, and we spent the next few hours trading swizzle sticks, travel stories, and pictures of our lives back home.

David looked about fifty, Corbin ten years younger. They lived in a Dallas suburb and had two passions: travel and tulips. Every fall they planted over 2000 bulbs, then threw a huge party when the tulips came up in the spring.

Ron told the group we were retired and went to Europe six weeks or more each year. This time it was Croatia, Bosnia and Montenegro.

"Montenegro!" said Naomi. "What's that supposed to be like?"

"Mountains, beaches.... We'll find out more and let you know," I replied. She gave me her email address.

David described in detail how he organized their trips, while Corbin ran around the roof introducing himself to the waiter and all the other customers.

With every round of drinks, our voices and raucous laughter got louder. Couples looking for a quiet evening left. Soon we were the only ones on the roof.

The group grew calm as we watched the sun go down, painting the sky in shades of orange and rose. Through gaps in the tower's castellated wall, I saw a small boat chugging from the harbor to a cruise ship several miles offshore. The last rays of sun were reflected in its wake.

We lingered over drinks. None of us wanted to leave the cross-roads that had brought us together. But by eight o'clock the wind had picked up and our group began to disperse. We hugged each other, Corbin hugged the waiter, and our new friends disappeared through the hole.

Ron and I were the last to leave. When I made it down and looked around the room, I saw people laughing. It was then

I realized that for the locals, we were the entertainment. Watching tourists climb up to the roof and down again was the highlight of their day.

Montenegro

Small Miracle in Montenegro

"Don't...talk," said Ron, his voice low and steady.

I glanced at my husband. He was staring at the road and holding the steering wheel tightly. All the color had left his face. I saw a curve and a dropoff and knew we were in trouble.

The day before on the bus to Montenegro, I had opened our guidebook to a picture of a large church built right into the face of a cliff.

"Look at this," I'd said to Ron, pointing to the photo.

"Whoa...is that real?" he asked. "What is it?"

"The Monastery of Ostrog," I said. "I'll find out more about it."

As I read further, I learned that the monastery was built in the seventeenth century by St. Basil, a Serbian Orthodox bishop who led the fight for Serbian independence. He and his followers carried rocks to the Ostrog caves, 900 meters above sea level, and built the church inside.

Basil's remains have been kept there since 1671. Orthodox, Catholic and Muslim pilgrims come from around the world to visit the holy place, and they all believe St. Basil brings miracles to the faithful. Many visitors pray to be healed or relieved of hardship. Witnesses tell of those who have regained the power of sight, overcome mental illness, or found comfort in dealing with loss.

I found it hard to believe the stories about miracles, but I wanted to see the impressive monastery.

Ron and I picked up our rented Opel the next morning. The guidebook had advised taking a bus to Ostrog, since the drive could be challenging. But we'd missed the last bus and were scheduled to leave the area the next day.

"Do you think we could drive up there?" I asked Ron.

"Sure," he said. "How hard could it be?"

We drove west from Podgorica for thirty miles before leaving the main road and heading up the mountain. As we passed little stands where farmers sold honey, figs and wine, it started to rain.

Gravel crunched under our wheels and pebbles trickled down a cliff from the road above. A single lane carried vehicles in both directions, with one hairpin turn after another and few chances to pull over and let others pass. I couldn't imagine meeting another car on that road, not to mention the bus Ron had seen high above us, making its way down.

The higher we went the more often I held my breath and gripped my seat. No guardrails or vegetation lined the roadway to keep cars from going over the edge, and at places the ground beneath the road had eroded. I tried to look for oncoming cars, but there was no way to see what was coming.

My throat went dry. "Boy, that's a long way down," I croaked.

That's when Ron told me not to talk. I felt even more scared and clung to the legend that no one had ever died on the monastery road.

After another sharp turn I looked up and gasped. Still high above us, on an almost vertical background, sat the gleaming white monastery. A few rays of sun shone through the clouds, lighting up the site and the rock around it. Ron glanced up and stopped the car. We stared at the church in wonder, and a calmness came over us. Like the pilgrims who'd been drawn there for centuries, I felt sure we would make it safely up the mountain.

As we sat on the side of the road, a bus passed going in the opposite direction, hardly slowing down. My fear returned, but a magnet was pulling us upward. A couple of miles later we were there. It had taken forty minutes to drive five miles.

We parked next to a dozen other vehicles, and I realized how lucky we'd been not to encounter more drivers. Getting out of the car I almost shouted for joy, but restrained myself when I saw several women praying near a fountain of holy water.

Ron and I went through a gate. The monastery loomed in front of us, lodged in the rock, with hundreds of meters of sheer cliff above and below. I agreed with the words on the Destination Montenegro website: "When you stand in front of the Monastery of Ostrog, your first thought will be that this is not the work of men."

The complex had two main buildings. The first, topped by arches and colorful frescoes, held monastic residences and lodging for pilgrims. In a small room at ground level, candles burned. A sign said visitors could light them, one side for the living, the other for the dead.

Farther up the hill was St. Basil's original church, its stone wall flush with the towering cliff. The sanctuary was inside, built into a cave. Ron and I passed through the door, shivering as we entered the cold, damp space. We could barely see the books and artifacts displayed in the dim light that filtered through several small windows.

Icons hung on the walls where pilgrims had tucked tiny notes and coins among the stones. I'd read that over centuries believers had left them, hoping for miracles. We wandered into a chapel, twelve feet long and eight feet wide, containing St. Basil's remains. Just outside, a young, black-robed priest padded silently among the visitors and disappeared behind a door.

Ron and I climbed up the stairs and stepped onto a balcony, blinking in the sunshine and breathing the clear mountain air. The Zeta River and Bjelopavlici Plain were spread out below, with forests, orchards and fields of wheat. We stayed for a few minutes to take in the view. Retracing our steps, we went back downstairs and left the church. I looked up and saw a simple white cross on top of the cliff, stark against the clear blue sky.

I was in awe of this place, preserved for centuries, giving hope and support to people of many faiths. Despite my skepticism, I felt connected to something larger than myself and filled with a sense of peace.

As we drove slowly down the mountain, I thought of the thousands of pilgrims who had made it safely over the narrow, winding road, seeking comfort and grace. It was enough to make me believe in miracles.

Montenegro

How to Trust a Teenager

ONE NIGHT IN MONTENEGRO I began to wonder if talking to strangers was always a good idea.

We were in Podgorica, the capital, where streets were packed with drivers following too closely, blaring their horns and cutting us off at every turn. The lack of street signs made it hard to find our hotel. When we hit a traffic circle, Ron went around a few times, took a guess and sped off.

After a long stretch of empty road with no landmarks, we headed up a hill and landed in a maze of narrow, winding streets lined with similar houses. The dark neighborhood looked deserted and we were the only car in sight. Ron drove randomly, growing more frustrated with every turn.

"Slow down," I said. "I'm trying to keep track of where we've been."

Ron peered out the windows. "Well, I'm looking for a street sign so we can call the hotel and ask them to send a taxi for us."

Just then he made a turn and drove down a steep alley.

"Uh-oh," I said. "A dead end."

"Damn it – no room to turn around," he said. Backing up in

137

the darkness seemed impossible. I sensed Ron was starting to panic.

"It's OK," I said quietly. "Just pull over. We can always wait until dawn, then walk up and get some help."

"Right, spend the night here, trapped," Ron said. "How about walking out now?"

"I don't know," I said. "We might wander off the road." Leaving the asphalt could mean stepping on a land mine from the 1990s Balkans War.

I climbed out of the car and glanced around. "Wait here," I said. "I'll look for a way out." Walking a few hundred feet, I peeked around a bend and saw a narrow lane that looked promising. I gave Ron a thumbs up, ran back to the car and got in. He inched forward and turned onto the slightly wider road, relieved to be out of the alley.

We drove aimlessly for another half hour, then encountered the only people we had seen that night, a couple of guys standing under a rare street light, smoking. They wore black vinyl jackets and combat boots.

"Should I stop?" Ron asked. "Maybe they can help us."

"Yeah," I said. "Or...."

"Well, I don't know what else to do." He parked, and we both got out of the car.

The boys were in their late teens, one slightly built with spiky blond hair, the other a bit taller and heavier. They spoke to each other quietly in Serbian, glancing at us a few times. But they never smiled.

"English?" I asked. They shook their heads. I held up a map, shrugged my shoulders and looked around. Ron handed the big guy a pen, hoping he would show us where we were. He drew an X on the map, and I was stunned to see we were over twenty miles from the city.

I marked the location of our hotel, thinking they could show us how to get there. But they didn't seem inclined to help. They started to argue, with one speaking and the other shaking his head no.

The blond kid pulled out a cell phone and made a call. He spoke urgently for a few minutes, then hung up and talked to his friend while gesturing at our rented Renault.

"Let's get out of here," I said.

"It's too late – they know how to find us," said Ron.

Suddenly a third man roared up on a large black motorcycle, the first moving vehicle we had seen for hours. He was a few years older than the others, scruffy, with messy clothes and a cigarette dangling from his mouth. I flashed on a time in Barcelona when a biker slashed our tires, then robbed us on the side of the road.

The new guy swaggered over and spoke rapidly to the others, jerking his head toward our car. They both nodded and said "OK." He vroomed off on his cycle while the first two motioned for us to get in the car, then jumped in the back seat and pointed downhill. They looked serious and determined.

"Where are we going?" I asked Ron, feeling afraid.

"No idea," he said, pulling ahead. I wondered if for once we'd regret talking to strangers.

The boys leaned forward. "Left," said one, directing us into an alley, then a few seconds later, "Right." When Ron didn't turn at that moment, he raised his voice: "Right! Right!" Ron turned sharply into what looked like a driveway but turned out to be a short, narrow street. We kept going, back and forth, back and forth, descending the hillside. I felt like I was in a pinball machine.

About twenty minutes later, we reached a level, more populated area. Nothing looked familiar.

"Are we back in the city?" I asked Ron.

"Not sure," he answered nervously. I glanced in the back seat. The guys were staring out the windows, swiveling their heads, talking to each other in spurts.

"I think they're looking for something," I said.

"Or someone," Ron said. "Maybe their biker friend." My fear went up a notch.

I turned around and asked, "Podgorica?"

One of them nodded tentatively, but they didn't say anything. I wondered if "left" and "right" were the only English words they knew. They looked nervous, and I started to panic. Ron drove forward in silence.

Then out of nowhere I saw a pub we had been to the night before, a few blocks from our hotel. "Look where we are!" I said, weak with relief.

"I can't believe it," Ron said.

I started laughing. "It's good!" I said to the backseat drivers. "OK!" I felt the tension drain out of my body. Ron stopped the car.

The boys broke into smiles for the first time that night. I wanted to express my gratitude but couldn't speak their language. Ron offered them a few bills ("for taxi," he kept saying), but they drew back indignantly and said "*Ne*" (No). They stuck out their hands to shake ours, clearly proud to have completed their mission.

"How will they get home?" I asked Ron, as one kid flipped open his cell phone. A couple of minutes later the biker we'd seen before came around the corner with a second guy, each on a motorcycle that could carry another person.

The boys climbed out of our car and headed toward their friends. They would get home and so would we, our faith in strangers restored.

Montenegro

Beauty Parlor Bonding

I was walking along the bay in Kotor, Montenegro, when a sign caught my eye: *Frizerski Salon Nada* – "Hairdressers Hope" – a good harbinger if I ever saw one. The water in our cottage had shut off and I needed my hair done.

The shop was in an old stone house. Peeking in the window, I saw four salon chairs and two drying hoods. The beauty parlor was closed, but a note on the door listed days and hours.

I jotted them down and had turned to walk away when a small young woman emerged from the house. Her blond hair was closely cropped and she wore a simple white blouse and pale blue wraparound skirt.

"Do you speak English?" I asked.

She looked startled, held up a finger and darted back into the house. In a few minutes she returned with a middle-aged man who looked like he might be her father.

"I help you?" he asked with a heavy accent.

"Yes," I replied, pointing to my head. "I would like an appointment."

He gave me a blank look.

"Can you…" I pantomimed washing my hair, then held up one arm, grasping an imaginary hair dryer. "Rrrrrrr," I said. Next I moved my fingers like scissors and shook my head no. I remembered a stylist in Spain who spoke no English and gave me a buzz cut before I could stop her.

"Ah…yes. Come," he said.

I pointed to my watch and shrugged my shoulders.

"Tomorrow you come. Two o'clock," he said.

The next day the room was abuzz with half a dozen Montenegrin ladies chatting in Serbian, their animated voices laced with laughter. The middle-aged women looked relaxed in their loose-fitting dresses and flat shoes. A few were having their hair done, while the rest appeared to be there just to socialize.

"Irma," said one, nodding toward the doorway as I walked in. The young woman I'd met the day before rushed over, looking apologetic. She glanced at the clock and gestured toward the other ladies. Then she led me to a chair, put a pillow behind my back and offered me a bowl of candy. I took a piece, smiled broadly and said "It's OK." I wasn't in a rush.

The other women stopped talking and looked at me for a few seconds. Then they resumed their lively conversation.

Irma worked steadily, shampooing and cutting, drying and fluffing. One by one she transformed the women. Each let her friends admire her, then sat down to watch the rest of the show. They all had tinted hair teased into a bouffant style, finished with a heavy dose of hair spray. I felt a little nervous; would I end up with a hairstyle from the 1960s?

Suddenly a tall lady swept into the shop wearing a long beige and gold dress, matching shoes and pearl jewelry. She was perfectly made up and her big hair was cemented into place. The other women were speechless for a moment, then erupted in a chorus of admiration. Someone leapt out of her chair so the regal lady could sit down and get a touchup from Irma. I could tell she was dressed for a special occasion and wondered where she was going.

"Aha," I thought. "She's the mother of the bride, or groom. They all know her and are going to the wedding." I longed to join in the conversation, find out more and tell them about my son's wedding the next month.

The fancy woman left ten minutes later in a flurry of excitement. Then it was my turn. I lay back in a salon chair and let the warm water pour over my head. Irma massaged my scalp. I relaxed and stopped caring about how my hair would turn out.

In the end I had a natural, layered style that might have appeared in an American magazine. The remaining ladies oohed and aahed over me.

Irma looked exhausted, her own hair plastered to her face, her posture slumped and eyes half-closed, and she still had two people to work on. She must have been standing all day. I paid her and tried to express my thanks for her hard work.

Then I walked out the door, feeling renewed and grateful for the company of women.

Kotor, Montenegro, May 2010

A curtain moves in the window
of an old stone building.
The empty one, I think,
my spine shivering –
who or what lives in the cottage next door?

I move to the water's edge,
gaze across the fjord at the town
closed for the night.
The medieval wall rises high against the hills
and shelters timeless buildings below.

Now in the darkness, lanterns on the wall
draw a circle of light
melting on the town
spreading on the water
setting fire to the tips of tiny waves
coming to my shore.

Dazzled,
I turn back to my lodging,
stumbling in the dark.
A light goes on
next door, outside the silent cottage,
just for me.
Just in time.

Bosnia & Herzegovina

Window of Opportunity

DURING THE 1990s BOSNIAN WAR, Serbian Nationalists attacked Sarajevo and laid siege to the city, blocking access to water, food and fuel supplies. They thought they could take Sarajevo in a few weeks, but its citizens held on for four years.

Sarajevans defied the enemy by going on with their normal routines. They went to work, though their offices were in shambles. Doctors and nurses toiled for no pay with limited medical supplies. Men and women got married and started families. Teachers set up makeshift schools in basements and staged a ballet – Ravel's Bolero, because the piece is usually danced barefoot and most of the dancers no longer had shoes.

Families scavenged for food and walked miles for water. They burned clothing, curtains, anything combustible to cook and stay warm. Every time a building was bombed, they used the wreckage as firewood.

Throughout their ordeal, Sarajevans shared what they had with each other, no matter their culture or religion. They fed the weakest first: the sick, elderly and mothers with babies. The people of Sarajevo held onto their humanity.

After the war ended in December 1995, most Bosnians put the

past behind them and moved forward with hope and purpose. Ron and I witnessed their warmth and good will during our three visits there between 2008 and 2012. People we met were open, generous, and thrilled we were visiting Sarajevo. Once we asked a man if he could point us to an Internet café, and he walked with us for forty-five minutes to show us the best in the city. On the way, he talked about Sarajevo and answered our questions. He described the city's resurgence after the war and told us how people of different religions were back living and working together, even inter-marrying.

We met those who had lost their childhoods or fought on the front lines but were full of optimism about the future. They were kind, high-spirited people, always ready for a good time.

On our first trip to Sarajevo, Ron saw a sign outside The Celtic Pub saying "60s and 70s Night on Wednesday." We had a penchant for Irish bars and had loved rock 'n roll dancing since we'd met thirty years earlier. Ron and I decided to go.

We got there early and grabbed a table near an open window. Ron ordered beers and we relaxed and took in the scene. I glanced out to the patio, where a couple caught my attention. The man was about thirty-five, with stubble on his face and short disheveled hair. He looked as tired as the worn-out shirt he was wearing. His friend, a blonde in her twenties, wore delicate gold earrings and a lime green tank top that set off her flawless skin.

Clearly upset, the girl was talking fervently and moving her clenched fist up and down. Her companion leaned forward, listening intently. Five or six empty mugs and a full ashtray sat between them.

"Something's happening with them," I said, watching the couple. "She seems upset."

"Maybe she's breaking up with him," Ron guessed. "Or vice versa."

"Hmm, I don't know. He could be her best friend...." I wasn't sure why, but I really cared about them.

A DJ arrived and started spinning oldies. Little by little, the bar filled up with locals, mostly in their thirties, who danced among the tables. We held back until they played "Brown Sugar," then jumped up and joined them. A few songs later we managed a jitterbug, and other dancers cheered to see people their parents' age dancing.

We sat down to rest and glanced outside. The young woman was speaking more calmly and even gave her friend a smile. The guy leaned back in his chair.

About ten o'clock, a waiter came up and closed the shutters between the patio and us. "Too much noise. Late for neighbors," he muttered.

It was as if someone had switched off a TV. As the mystery couple disappeared, I gave them a secret little wave. "I guess we'll never find out their story," I said.

The music drew us back in. A flamenco version of "Please Don't Let Me Be Misunderstood" had everyone dancing. Then, during a sultry *"Bésame Mucho,"* Ron and I clung to each other and twirled around, swept away by the music.

Around midnight Ron signaled to the waiter. "We'd like to cash out," he said.

"But...." The waiter looked bewildered. "Someone bought these for you." He nodded at the beers on his tray.

"Who?" I asked, glancing at Ron. "We don't know anyone here."

"Them."

Ron and I looked in the direction he was pointing and saw the couple from the patio, who had moved inside. We were dumbfounded.

The guy lifted his hand slightly, nodded and gave us a small smile. We were delighted and went right over to meet them.

"Hello," he said, "I am Adnan Spaho, and this is my wife, Irma." Like most Sarajevans under forty, they spoke English fluently. We thanked them for the beers and introduced ourselves.

Their whole mood had changed. Irma was relaxed and her husband looked energized. "Where are you from?" he asked.

"The U.S.," said Ron. "Seattle."

"Ahh... great, I thought so," Adnan said.

For the next few hours, we chatted like old friends. They asked about our trip and were pleased to hear we had spent two weeks in Sarajevo.

Irma's face lit up when we asked about their family. "We have a son, Affan. He's three and a half and very smart. Adnan's parents are taking care of him tonight," she said.

"We have a boy, too," I smiled. "But he just turned thirty-two."

Adnan told us about their small cleaning business and how hard it was to find good workers. They had gone to the pub so Irma could vent her frustration.

Ron and I glanced at each other. So that was it.

The music made it hard to talk, but we felt a strong connection. They said they had watched us dancing and were inspired by how sympatico we looked. Ron even got Adnan to dance. ("He never dances!" Irma said.)

We finally left the pub about two a.m. They invited us for a barbecue at their house the following evening. "Adnan can pick you up," Irma said.

At six the next day her husband came to get us, racing down

a hill in a yellow Citroen convertible, grinning from ear to ear. We jumped in the little car and sputtered up the hill. Five minutes later Irma greeted us in their driveway.

Adnan proudly showed off "Yellow Thunder," a carefully restored 1967 2CV model. Citroens were rare in Bosnia, and this one was in perfect condition. Adnan and Irma stood next to the car, posing for pictures like proud parents.

On the patio, Adnan brought us beer while Irma put *cevapi* and green peppers on the grill. The crackling sausages smelled delicious. Their son Affan, slight with big brown eyes, ran around the lawn, stopping from time to time to grab a bite of meat and glance at us sideways.

Over dinner, we talked about the Bosnian War that had ended only ten years before. Bombs had fallen in the now-peaceful neighborhood. Adnan told us that when he wasn't on the front lines, he fixed Citroens for use in the conflict. I pictured the little cars buzzing around, dodging bullets as they carried their precious cargo of people and supplies.

When it got dark, we went up to the family apartment. Ron and I stopped short in the doorway and started to laugh. I knew Adnan loved Citroens, but I wasn't prepared for the shrine I saw in their living room. He had cut the body of an older 2CV in half lengthwise, painted it silver, and put it against a red wall with a candelabra on top.

"Wow," said Ron.

"I know," Adnan said with a smile. "Beautiful, isn't it? Irma had her doubts at first, but…."

Irma, Ron and I relaxed while Affan played and Adnan moved around the apartment, collecting CDs of Bosnian music for us to take home. He also made a copy of a Bosnian War documentary featuring Adnan and his father zipping around in a battered Citroen.

Before I knew it, four hours had passed. We started to say our goodbyes, and they begged us to go back to the Celtic the next night. "Friday is great there," Irma said.

"I don't know," I said. "Ron may have to go without me. I have to pack and clean the apartment."

"But it's your last night in Sarajevo," Adnan said.

"I'll try my best," I said, not feeling too hopeful.

Ron and I spent the next day finding handmade slippers, jewelry and other crafts to take home. Late that afternoon Ron went for a walk and I tried to figure out how to fit our stuff into two small backpacks. As I sorted and packed, I kept thinking about Irma and Adnan.

Then I stopped. "What am I doing?" I asked myself, heading for the shower. "Who knows when we'll see them again?"

As soon as Ron got back, I announced, "I'm going."

"I thought you'd see the light. We can clean the place later."

I tossed on a T-shirt displaying Wolfie, symbol of the 1984 Olympic Games, Sarajevo's proudest moment. We got to the Celtic by eight and found Adnan and Irma right away. "You made it!" Adnan exclaimed, beaming.

"We brought Affan," Irma said. "He's never been to a pub before." He was already a hit with all the young women.

Before long the music started, and, as usual, Ron went wild on the dance floor. He wore me out, then Irma. Other dancers asked Ron to join them, amazed at his energy.

Around midnight Affan finally got tired and crawled onto his mother's lap. We left the pub and our friends walked us back to our hostel. The old town was dark except for a light coming from a small window in an old house. Irma stopped and bought three bags of fresh pastries.

"You have to try these – in Sarajevo we always eat them after drinking," she said.

One bag was to enjoy together, one they would keep, and one was for us to take on our journey. The delicacy tasted sweet and salty, like a cross between a doughnut and a pretzel.

The five of us stood in the empty street munching our treats, not saying much. We had only known each other for three days, but already felt a strong bond. Even little Affan looked sad. His father made us promise to return to Sarajevo, and we told them we'd be back. Then we parted.

Ron and I climbed the stairs to our apartment. He cleaned as I threw our stuff into backpacks. Then we fell into bed.

A few hours later, we grabbed a cab to the airport. As we waited for our flight to Dubrovnik, Ron and I started planning our next visit.

We went back to Sarajevo twice more. At the end of our third visit, Ron and I were back in the Celtic Pub with Irma, Adnan and Affan. We had just spent an overnight in Pocitelj exploring the ruins of a fortified hill town. I was telling our friends all about it when Ron's cell phone rang.

He flipped it open, waited a bit and said: "Sorry, I can't understand.... Do you...English?" He almost hung up, then handed the phone to Adnan, who spoke to the caller in Bosnian. His face grew serious. Holding the phone to the side, he leaned across the table and looked straight at Ron.

"They have your passports," he said. The color drained out of Ron's face.

Adnan talked into the phone and listened, then walked outside and paced back and forth, pressing the phone to his ear.

Irma sensed our anxiety and spoke in a calm, level voice: "Don't worry. We will solve the problem. We will get your passports."

She joined her husband outside and he paused to fill her in. Irma nodded and held out her hand. When Adnan gave her the phone, she started walking in circles and talking emphatically, moving her fist up and down.

Adnan came back inside and sat down with us.

"Is it the place we stayed near Pocitelj?" I asked nervously.

"Yes, they took your passports when you checked in and forgot to give them back."

"And we forgot to retrieve them," Ron said, his shoulders sagging.

Pocitelj was almost three hours away over a mountain range. It was eight thirty at night, and we were scheduled to fly to Athens at six thirty the next morning.

It seemed like a miracle when Irma and Adnan came up with a plan. The hotel owner, filled with remorse, had agreed to meet Adnan halfway between Pocitelj and Sarajevo to deliver our passports that night. Irma insisted the man drive two thirds of the way to Sarajevo, since it was "two thirds his fault." Besides, Adnan's drive over the mountains would be slower and more treacherous.

By nine o'clock Adnan was in his car, racing toward the meeting place. In true Bosnian fashion, when the men met they had coffee and made plans to get together with their families.

Adnan returned to Sarajevo about one a.m. We all had a nightcap, listened to Bosnian music and talked until we left for the airport at four o'clock that morning.

Flying to Greece, Ron and I reminisced about our first connection with the Spahos – through an open window – and how our friendship and love had deepened over the years.

Just like other Bosnians during the war, Adnan and Irma were determined to solve the problem we were facing and strong enough to make it happen. This was the spirit that enabled Sarajevans to defend and preserve the city they loved. We saw it come to life in their beloved Celtic Pub when everyone sang and danced to their disco anthem, "I Will Survive."

Acknowledgments

Many thanks to everyone who encouraged me to write travel stories and turn them into a book.

I appreciate the support of my remarkable writing group: Debra Daniels-Zeller, Kathy Gehrt, Wendy Hinman, Elsie Hulsizer, Sheila Kelly and Sharon Morris.

Frances Robinson, book designer and editor, played an essential role in publishing this collection. Her talent and skill made it all come together.

I am thankful to Larry Habegger, Executive Editor of Travelers' Tales, who encouraged me to share my stories with the world. Robert Mottram read my manuscript and gave me valuable insight and advice.

Here's to Ron, who shares my passion for independent travel and makes it a priority in our lives. Our son Dan cheers me on when I write, and grandson Maxwell draws us back home.

Finally, to all the people I've met on my travels, who made places come alive, became friends and enriched our lives, I am profoundly grateful.